MONEY M8

Jonquil Lowe

WHICH? BOOKS   CONSUMERS' ASSOCIATION

Which? Books are commissioned by
Consumers' Association and published by
Which? Ltd, 2 Marylebone Road, London NW1 4DF
Email: books@which.net

Distributed by The Penguin Group:
Penguin Books Ltd, 80 Strand, London WC2R 0RL

First edition March 2004

Copyright © 2004 Which? Ltd

British Library Cataloguing in Publication Data
A catalogue record for *Money M8* is available from the British Library

ISBN 0 85202 978 0

Editorial and production: Joanna Bregosz, Nithya Rae, Jennifer Steele
Index: Marie Lorimer
Original cover concept by Sarah Harmer
Cover photograph by Digital Vision/getty images

Typeset by Saxon Graphics Ltd, Derby
Printed and bound in England by Clays Ltd, St Ives plc

Contents

	Introduction	7
1	Getting a bank account	9
2	Using your bank account	18
3	Budgeting	35
4	Borrowing	42
5	Plastic fantastic?	51
6	Coping with debt	63
7	Savings and investments	72
8	Getting a job: your rights	86
9	Understanding your pay slip	94
10	Your finances as a student	106
11	Insuring your possessions	118
12	Car insurance	130
13	Holiday money	141
14	Travel insurance	155
	Useful contacts★	167
	Index	173

★ An asterisk next to the name of an organisation in the text indicates that contact details and websites can be found in this section

Introduction

Having money is great. Spending it is a doddle. Sorting out your finances sounds like a bore. But the world is becoming ever more complex and, increasingly, governments expect you to take financial responsibility for yourself. This is true whether you are thinking about financing your studies, wondering how best to save up, getting to grips with your first pay cheque, or guarding against life's little disasters.

The only way to be sure that you are making the right moves, getting the best deals and not being ripped off is to get some financial nous. The sooner you do this the better. The minute you start to get pocket money or a Saturday job, you are ready to play the financial system. By the time you start work or go to university, you should be firmly in control.

There is a lot of information out there about personal finance. You'll find myriad websites, finance pages in newspapers, specialist magazines, and so on. Which? Books itself publishes other guides on handling money wisely. But much of the material you'll come across is aimed at older adults and, though it's all good stuff, a lot of it is not so relevant when you are in your teens or early twenties. This book is different. It brings together the key information that is most likely to be useful to you now, given the financial problems and opportunities that you and other young people are likely to face.

Money M8 cuts through the jargon and gives you the lowdown on:

- opening and running bank and savings accounts
- handling credit
- solving debt problems if they do arise
- managing your finances as a student
- understanding your rights when you start work
- coping with the tax system

- the ins and outs of car insurance and possessions insurance
- guidance on money and insurance when you go travelling.

With examples and practical tips, this guide uses plain language to debunk personal finance and show how you can make the most of your money. It demonstrates how counting the pounds and pennies can be simple but effective – and perhaps even fun.

CHAPTER 1

Getting a bank account

Once you start a Saturday job or want to buy stuff on the Net, you will find that cash isn't very convenient and you need a bank account. Also, you can get your parents to pay any allowance direct to your account, avoiding all those 'I haven't the change right now/can you wait until…' delays.

In any case, when you become a student or start full-time work, a bank account becomes essential for receiving your student loan or wages. You don't have to stick with the bank you chose when you were younger. Banks see you as a potential customer for life and are very keen to woo you with all sorts of features and freebies, so it's well worth shopping around.

> Roar, one of the most extensive youth projects in the UK which provides continuous research into the lives of young people, found that nearly three-quarters of those aged 15 to 24 still have an account with the first bank they tried, but half this group now has another account as well.

Types of account

For day-to-day management of the money you get and spend, you need a current account. Until you reach 18, you'll almost certainly be limited to a basic bank account. Some of these are branded for young people and are often called 'youth accounts'.

From 18 onwards (21 with some more old-fashioned banks), you may be able to get a full current account, though this will depend on how the bank views your credit standing – see page 48. Most banks have in their range current accounts specifically aimed at students.

If you just want to put away some money, say, to pay for driving lessons or fund a holiday, you need a savings account – see Chapter 7.

Basic bank account

This type of account has the features you need for everyday transactions, but is designed to prevent you spending more money than you've got. So there is no chequebook and no over-draft facility.

Money can be paid in as cash, cheques or automated transfers (which just means that money is moved direct from someone else's bank account to yours). Examples of automated transfers include an employer paying your wages direct to your account or your parents arranging for an allowance to be paid in each month by standing order.

All basic bank accounts let you draw money out through cash machines using a plastic card. Most also let you pay for things using a debit card, or by setting up a standing order or direct debit to pay regular sums. However, very few accounts for under-16s include these extra features – Barclays and NatWest get a pat on the back for making a debit card available from age 11 onwards.

Unlike other types of current account, you often do not earn any interest on the money in a basic bank account. However, youth accounts usually do include interest.

What's a debit card?

A debit card is a plastic card that you can use to pay for things you buy or in a cash machine to get out money. The payment or withdrawal comes direct out of your bank account (which is very different from a credit card – see Chapter 5). A debit card is particularly handy because it lets you shop by phone and the Internet as well as in person.

Basic bank accounts come with a special sort of debit card (Solo or Electron), which involves the balance in your account being checked before each payment or withdrawal to see if there is enough money available. The transaction goes ahead only if there is enough, so there should be little risk of going over-drawn.

Standing orders and direct debits

A standing order is an instruction you give your bank to make a payment of the same amount at regular intervals (say, each month) direct to someone else's bank account. For example, you might use it to pay your rent. Equally, other people can use a standing order to make regular payments direct to your bank account.

A direct debit is a bit different. It is an instruction you give to your bank to allow someone else to draw agreed amounts from your account, usually at regular intervals. These days, direct debits are a very common way to pay any regular bill, such as magazine and club subscriptions or fuel and telephone bills. See Chapter 2 for more information about standing orders and direct debits.

Full current account

This has all the features of a basic bank account and more. In particular, you'll usually get a chequebook and cheque guarantee card. If you pay someone using a cheque with a guarantee card, your bank will honour the payment even if there is not enough money in your account. So it's really important to make sure you've got the money before you write the cheque, otherwise you'll go overdrawn.

Some full current accounts come with a small free overdraft (say, £50). But apart from that, if you go overdrawn without asking the bank first, you'll usually end up paying hefty charges. If you know you're likely to dip into the red, call your bank first to agree an overdraft, called an 'authorised overdraft', which will be cheaper.

With a full current account, you usually earn interest on the money you have in the account. But the big high-street banks mostly pay such a low rate of interest that it's hardly worth having. The highest rates tend to be paid by Internet banks.

Full current accounts aimed at students usually have additional features, such as larger interest-free overdrafts, relatively cheap authorised overdrafts and specialist advice services.

Choosing an account

How to shop around

There are two main ways to shop around for an account. You can do the legwork yourself by visiting local branches, phoning them to send you details, or visiting their websites. Alternatively, you can use the comparisons already made by someone else. When it comes to bank, building society and similar accounts, the main organisation that makes these kinds of comparison is Moneyfacts★. The information produced by Moneyfacts is also published in many newspapers, personal finance magazines and some websites, such as *www.support4learning.co.uk*.

What to look for

Access is important. Usually, you can withdraw money from any cash machine and, provided you stick to the machines in main locations, such as banks and large supermarkets, this is generally a free service. But you may have to pay if you use a machine at, say, a nightclub, petrol station or convenience store. With some accounts you can withdraw cash at Post Offices using your cash card.

Bear in mind that you might need physically to pay in money, for example a birthday cheque. Some cash machines let you pay in money, but many don't. So you might need to visit a branch. Consider when you can get there. If you are still at school, it may be hard to visit during the bank's opening hours (typically weekdays 9.30am to 4.30pm), unless it's open on Saturdays as well. There might be a bank operating some sort of service at your school. If you are a student, there will usually be a selection of banks on campus or nearby. A few full current accounts let you pay in at Post Offices, provided your bank has supplied you with the special paying-in slips that you'll need.

Consider how you want to operate your account. Some accounts are available only by Internet, phone or post. Some are branch-based. Others let you choose.

With a current account, consider what features you want. Do you need a debit card, standing orders, direct debits, cheque-book, overdraft, and so on? Current accounts, but seldom basic bank accounts, may pay interest on your account balance. However, unless you have a lot of money in the account, the amount of interest you receive – even at a good rate – is unlikely to be much. It is usually better to transfer any surplus to a savings account – see Chapter 7.

Accounts aimed at young people and students typically come with a range of freebies (see Table 1.1 for some examples). Don't let the goodies sway you unless the account definitely has the access and features you want.

A survey by Roar found that although 74 per cent of those aged 15 to 24 have access to the Internet, only 9 per cent with a bank account choose to bank online.

Table 1.1 Examples of freebies with youth and student accounts

Bank/building society	Account	Target age group	Free gifts/ incentives
NatWest	Card Plus	11–15	Free CD
Royal Bank of Scotland	Route 15	11–15	Personal organiser, discount on CDs, DVDs and computer games
Alliance & Leicester	Young Worker	16–17	Discounts on activities, DVDs and pizzas
Barclays	Youth	16–19	15% discount on Waterstone's vouchers
HSBC	Right Track Gap Year	16–17 18–19	Free BSM driving lesson if four others booked; free theory test question book
Royal Bank of Scotland	R21	16–21	Discounts on CDs, DVDs and concert tickets
Barclays	Student package	Students	Waterstone's and HMV vouchers and discounts on Waterstone's and HMV vouchers
HSBC	Student service	Students	Five-year railcard worth £90 or £50 cash
Lloyds TSB	Student account	Students	National Express card, Blackwell's discount, mobile phone deal, prize draw for payment of fees
NatWest	Student account	Students	£55 or £40 cash depending on where you open the account

Source: Moneyfacts, September 2003.

How to open a bank account

Check the details

Once you have narrowed down your choice of account, contact the bank or building society and ask it to provide details and an application form. Typically, you'll get a brochure summarising the account features. Somewhere there should also be a copy of the full terms and conditions. These might be in a separate leaflet or printed on the back of the application form – you can usually spot them by the very tiny print.

Dull though it seems, it is worth skimming through the terms and conditions. These include important features such as: how long it takes for money to become available for you to spend or draw out after you've paid it in (called the 'clearing' period); what happens if you accidentally go overdrawn; and what you are expected to do to keep the account secure (for example, looking after passwords and plastic cards). Charges and interest rates will usually be set out on a separate note but form part of the terms and conditions.

Make sure you are happy that the account offers what you want. If so, go ahead and complete the application form. If you are applying for an Internet account, you can usually fill in and submit the application form online.

Proving who you are

Banks and building societies are required by law to check the identity and address of new customers. This is to guard against criminals opening accounts under fake names and then using the accounts to make money from drugs and other crimes look as if it has come from legitimate sources (a practice called money laundering).

You'll be asked to produce two documents – one to prove who you are and the other to prove where you live. You can't use the same document to prove both. Table 1.2 shows examples of documents that are usually acceptable, but each bank and building society makes its own rules. Official documents tend to be preferred. The snag is: if this is your first account, you might not have two of these documents. In that case, talk to the bank and it may be willing to accept other forms of proof, such as documents in a parent's name if you are under 16, or a personal assurance from a parent, a teacher or someone else who knows you well.

Usually, you'll need to visit a branch of the bank or building society to show your documents in person. The bank or building society will return them straight away after taking a photocopy. If you are opening an Internet, phone or postal account, you'll have to post the documents and they will be returned in a few days.

Table 1.2 Examples of documents usually acceptable as proof of who you are and where you live

To prove who you are:

Full UK passport
Identity Card if you are a from another European Union country
Student identity card
UK photocard driving licence
National Insurance card and a payslip
Birth certificate
NHS medical card
If under 18, introduction from parent or guardian who is an existing customer

To prove where you live:

UK photocard driving licence
Paid gas or electricity bill less than three months old
Paid phone bill less than three months old
Bank statement from another bank less than three months old
Vehicle registration document
Vehicle licence renewal notification
Car insurance certificate
UCAS letter showing your name and address
Student Loan Company award letter
University/college offer letter
University/college letter of acceptance or enrolment

Your rights as a bank customer

Most banks and building societies have agreed to abide by a voluntary code of practice called the Banking Code*. When you apply for an account, you will usually be given a brief leaflet about the code, but you can on request get a full copy of it. The Code sets out minimum standards of good practice which the bank or building society should observe in its dealings with you.

If you have a complaint about your bank or building society, you should first direct it to your usual branch. The bank or building society must have a formal complaints procedure and must tell you how to use this. If you are unhappy with the outcome of your complaint or your bank or building society takes longer than six months to respond, you can take your case to the Financial Ombudsman Service (FOS)★. This is an independent complaints body that is free to use and can order the bank or building society to put matters right and if appropriate pay you compensation.

It is very rare that a bank or building society goes bust. If it did, you might be able to claim compensation from the Financial Services Compensation Scheme (FSCS)★ for any money you lost. The maximum compensation is the full amount of the first £2,000 in your account plus 90 per cent of the next £33,000 (i.e., up to £31,700 in total).

CHAPTER 2

Using your bank account

Once the bank or building society has accepted your application, it will give you a welcome pack. This usually includes a guide to operating your account. But here is an outline of the basics and a few other tips you might consider.

Getting your money out

The first thing you learn about driving is how to stop the car. Similarly, your first concern with a bank account is usually: how do I get my money out?

Cash from machines

With most accounts, you'll be sent a cash card, which you should sign on the back immediately. Separately (for security reasons), you'll be sent a personal identification number (PIN), which you use to operate the card. It is very important that you keep your PIN secret and safe – see *Looking after PINs and passwords*, on page 23.

When you want to withdraw cash, find a machine and insert your card in the slot, usually face up and with the top of the card to the right. Follow the on-screen instructions. The smallest note a cash machine dispenses is usually £10. So the smallest amount you can withdraw is £10 and any other withdrawal must be a multiple of £10.

To ensure you have access to the last few pounds in your account, most banks let you draw out a last £10 from a cash machine even if you have slightly less than that in your account. But, in that case, you will go overdrawn and, depending on the terms and conditions of the account, you may have to pay over-

draft charges. This applies even if you have a basic bank account (specifically designed to guard against going overdrawn). It is still your responsibility to keep track of the money in your account and to avoid becoming overdrawn.

Cash machines often ask if you want a receipt. This can be useful to help you keep track of your money. But make sure you keep receipts safe and never throw them away near a cash machine, which is an obvious hunting ground for fraudsters who can often make use of the information on receipts.

The Lebanese loop

Be suspicious if your card is hard to insert in a cash machine slot or is retained by the machine. You could be the victim of a device called the 'Lebanese loop'. This is a piece of plastic that a thief places in the card slot. Your card appears to have been retained, but, once you walk away, the thief releases the loop with your card inside. The thief will then go shopping with your card or, if he or she has managed to overlook you as you tried to key in your PIN, may take cash direct from your account.

If your card is retained by a machine, the safest course is to notify the card issuer at once to put a stop on the card. It's a good idea to carry with you the card issuer's emergency number and, if you have a mobile, ring up while you are still by the machine.

Cash from a Post Office

Some banks and one building society have made arrangements so that current and basic bank account customers can make withdrawals at Post Offices. You present your cash or debit card, tell the cashier how much you want to withdraw, and key your PIN into the keypad on the counter. The cashier then hands you the money.

Unlike cash machines (see above), you can withdraw less than £10 at Post Offices, thereby giving you access to the last few pounds in your account without going overdrawn. You can also withdraw any amount, not just multiples of £10.

Cash from a supermarket

If you are buying goods in a supermarket using a debit card, you can usually also take advantage of 'cashback'. You simply ask the cashier to let you have cash up to £50. The cashier pays you with money from the till. The withdrawal is shown on your till receipt and subtracted direct from your bank account along with the payment for the goods you bought.

Paying with a debit card

If you are in a shop that accepts your type of card, you can pay for goods or services with your debit card. Most shops have pictures of the logos of the cards they accept, perhaps on the door or beside the till. If you're not sure whether your card is accepted, ask before you start to shop.

Solo and Electron cards are often not accepted where you use up the goods or services before payment – for example, in a restaurant or at a filling station. This is because of the risk to the retailer that there will not be enough money in your account to pay for goods that you've already had. You'll also find that not all websites accept Solo and Electron cards even though they may accept other types of debit card.

When paying in a shop, you hand over your card, which is then inserted in a machine that dials up your bank to obtain authorisation for the transaction. If you are using a Solo or Electron card, this process includes checking the balance in your account to make sure there is enough money left to cover your latest purchase. If authorised, currently the machine prints out a payment slip which you are asked to sign. The shop assistant checks that your signature matches that on the card, returns the card to you and gives you one part of the payment slip as a receipt. You should keep the receipts and use them to help you check your statements (see pages 33–4). Signing a payment slip is being phased out and increasingly you will be asked instead to key your PIN number into a pad.

If you buy over the phone or Internet, obviously you can't sign a slip. You'll be asked to give the details embossed on the front of the card – typically the name of the cardholder, the card number, expiry date and sometimes an issue number and start date. You should normally also be asked for a three-digit security number. This is the last three digits of the number on the back of the card on the signature strip. You will never be asked to state your PIN and under no circumstances should you ever tell it to anyone.

Example

Tim buys a domain name from an Internet site. It costs £11.99 for two years and he wants to pay by Solo card. The website asks him to key in his card details. First, Tim makes sure that this is being done over a secure link by checking that the web address starts with 'https'. The link is secure, so he keys in the name on his card, his card number, issue number, expiry date and the last three digits of the security number from the reverse of the card.

Chart 2.1 The card details you usually have to give when paying by phone or the Internet

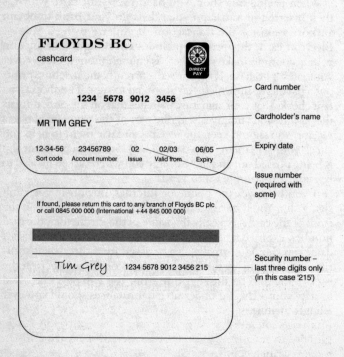

Looking after PINs and passwords

- Try to memorise all PINs (used with plastic cards) and passwords (used for phone and Internet banking).
- Destroy the slip telling you a PIN or password.
- Never write your PIN on the card or keep a note of the PIN with the card.
- If you must write down PINs or passwords, make sure they are disguised. (But be aware that crooks will go through a whole address book trying out combinations from phone numbers to see if they are disguised PINs.)
- You can change PINs (at cash machines) or passwords to something you find easier to remember. But avoid obvious combinations that could easily be guessed by other people, such as your birth date, house or phone numbers, 1234, 6666, and so on.
- Never tell anyone your PIN or password. No genuine official will ever ask you for your PIN or your whole password.
- Tell the card issuer, bank or building society immediately if you suspect any misuse of your card, PIN or password.

Paying by standing order

Ask your bank to give you a form (or use the online form if you are Internet banking). You'll have to write in:

- the name of the person you want to pay (sometimes called the 'beneficiary')
- the sort code of his or her bank or building society (a unique number identifying the branch)
- his or her bank or building society account number
- the amount you want to pay
- when and how often you want to pay
- when payments should start
- when the payments should stop (or alternatively that they are to continue until you tell your bank otherwise).

Return the form to your bank. It usually takes a few days to set up the standing order. Alternatively, your bank may be happy initially to set up a standing order by phone, but will then require written confirmation.

Although each payment will leave your account on the stated day, it may take a few days (usually at least three working days) to reach the account of the person you are paying. The terms and conditions should say how long it will take – if not, ask your bank.

If you want to alter or cancel a standing order, you should again ask your bank for a form to fill in with your new instructions.

Example

Julie rents a room in a private house. Her rent is £250 due on the first day of each month. Julie drops into her bank, Floyds Banking Corporation, and asks for a standing order form. She fills this in, asking her landlady for her bank account details. Julie instructs the bank to make the payment on the twenty-fifth day of each month. This allows for the three working days that the bank says it may take for the money to reach her landlady's account.

Paying by direct debit

If you want to pay a regular bill by direct debit, you can ask your bank to set this up, although more often the firm you want to pay will give you a form (often called a mandate or instruction) to fill in. The form is an instruction to your bank to allow the firm to take the necessary payments from your account. You usually return the form to the firm (rather than your bank). The firm will then pass the form to your bank together with its bank account details.

Most are 'variable direct debits', which means that the firm can alter the amount it collects from your account without you having to sign a new form. But the firm must give you notice (usually at least ten days) of the changed amount, so that you have time to object if you do not agree to the increase.

Although you arrange the direct debit with the firm you are paying, your bank or building society is responsible for monitoring the payments and putting right any problems. So if, say, the wrong amount is paid under the direct debit or a payment is taken when none should have been, you complain to your bank or building society. You are guaranteed a full and immediate refund from your bank or building society of any amounts paid in error.

To cancel a direct debit, tell your bank or building society. Do this in writing and keep a copy as a record of your instruction. It's courteous to tell the firm you were paying that you are cancelling the direct debit, so that it can close your account.

Direct debits are commonly used to pay, for example, phone bills, fuel bills, insurance premiums, sports club subscriptions, and so on.

Paying bills monthly

If you are starting to pay fuel and phone bills for the first time, the supplier might insist that you pay monthly in advance by direct debit. The usual alternative is to pay quarterly in arrears (i.e., after you have used the service), but suppliers are reluctant to allow this if you have not yet built up a credit record to show that you can be trusted to pay.

The direct debit is usually set up so that you pay a set amount each month. This is set high enough to cover your expected quarterly bill. In fact, the firm usually errs in its favour and sets your payment a bit too high, so you may find you build up a surplus in the account. You can ask for repayment of any surplus and for your monthly payments to be reduced, though you may have to be persistent as some firms are very slow to make refunds or adjustments. If you have problems, complain to Energywatch*.

Fuel and phone companies might offer you a small discount if you agree to pay by direct debit. By contrast, if you arrange to pay for something like car insurance or possessions insurance monthly by direct debit instead of paying a single lump sum up front, you may be charged extra.

Example

Rick moves into his first flat and contacts the electricity supplier to change the account to his name. The supplier estimates that each quarter Rick will use about £40 of electricity. It insists he pays monthly by direct debit and sets his payments at £15 a month. After three months, Rick has paid 3 × £15 = £45. His first quarterly bill is £37.05. This is deducted from his account, leaving £45 − £37.05 = £7.95 surplus to be carried forward.

Paying by cheque

If you have a full current account, you will usually be given a chequebook which you can use to make payments from your account. Cheques have become a bit outdated if you are buying something in person – it's usually easier to use a debit card (or possibly a credit card – see Chapter 7). But cheques can be handy if, for example, you need to send a payment through the post.

Shops and other retailers are often reluctant to accept a cheque unless you have a cheque guarantee card. Without a guarantee card, the cheque might 'bounce' (be rejected by your bank) if there is not enough money in your account to cover the payment. With a guarantee card, the payment goes ahead regardless of the amount in your account. The card guarantees cheques only up to a set amount shown on your card – usually £50, £100 or £200. The guarantee is valid only for a single cheque per transaction, so you can't guarantee a higher amount by paying for a more expensive item with, say, two cheques.

Writing a cheque is straightforward – see Chart 2.2. Try to write right up to the edge of the spaces provided and put a line through any bits left blank – this makes it harder for anyone to alter what you have written. If you make a mistake, it's usually best to destroy the cheque and start again. Alternatively, you can correct a mistake, but you should then initial the correction.

If you have an account with the organisation you are paying – for example, a fuel supplier or credit-card provider – for added security, you can write your account or customer number on the pay line immediately after the name of the firm.

Most cheques these days are already printed with crossed lines and the words 'account payee'. These are security measures to prevent cheques you've written being misused if they are lost or stolen. The crossing means the cheque must be paid into a bank account. 'Account payee' means it must be the account of the person named on the pay line. If, unusually, your cheques are not already printed this way, draw in the crossings yourself, add 'account payee' and ask your bank to provide you with printed crossed cheques in future.

You can use a cheque to draw out cash, in which case write 'Cash' on the pay line.

Make sure you fill in the stub/record chart in your cheque-book with the date, the person/firm you paid and the amount paid. This is your record of the payment which you should use in order to keep track of your account (see pages 33–4).

Post-dated cheques

Usually, the date you write on a cheque will be the current date. However, you can put a future date if you want the payment to be delayed until later – this is called writing a post-dated cheque. University halls of residence, for example, are often happy to accept payment for the whole year in the form of several post-dated cheques to be paid at the start of each term.

Be careful to whom you give post-dated cheques. If the person it's made out to pays in the cheque early, your bank may well make the payment regardless of the date. Although this would be an error on the part of the bank, complaining and sorting out any knock-on effects (such as overdraft charges and other payments bouncing) would be a hassle. So make sure that anyone you give a post-dated cheque to is clear about not presenting the cheque to his or her bank before the date written on the cheque.

Example

To celebrate her boyfriend's birthday, Julie takes him out for a meal at a local American-Italian restaurant. She pays for the meal by cheque, written out as shown in Chart 2.2 (see overleaf).

Chart 2.2 How to write a cheque

On the pay line put the name of the person or firm you are paying (often called the payee). Julie writes the name of the restaurant

Write the amount you are paying in words and the same amount in figures in the box. The bill in Julie's case came to £32.22

Don't forget to write the date on the cheque

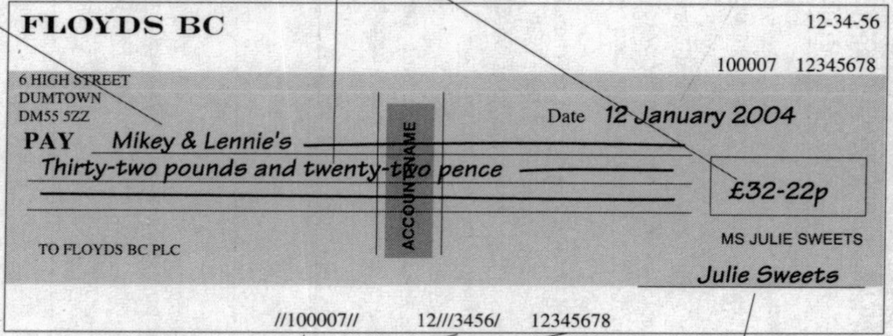

FLOYDS BC

6 HIGH STREET
DUMTOWN
DM55 5ZZ

12-34-56

100007   12345678

Date _12 January 2004_

PAY   _Mikey & Lennie's_

Thirty-two pounds and twenty-two pence

ACCOUNT NAME

£32-22p

TO FLOYDS BC PLC

//100007//   12//3456/   12345678

MS JULIE SWEETS

Julie Sweets

Sign the cheque

Numbers identifying the bank, account and cheque appear here and are repeated at the top of the cheque. In this case, the number of the cheque is 100007, the sort code of the bank (a unique code that identifies your particular bank branch) is 12-34-56 and the number of Julie's account is 12345678

Paying by bank draft

If you buy something big, such as a car, particularly from a private individual, the seller might be reluctant to accept your cheque in case it bounces. One way around this problem is to pay with a bank draft. Essentially, a bank draft is the bank's own cheque. Payment is guaranteed, so it can be treated virtually as cash.

You obtain a bank draft by asking at your bank. You may have to fill in a form and there is a charge (say, £10). You must have enough money in your account to cover the draft and the charge. The draft is made out to the person you want to pay and is signed on behalf of the bank. Your name does not appear on the draft and you do not sign it.

However, if you are selling something and are offered a bank draft, do take care. Sometimes criminals forge bank drafts, so take the draft to your own bank and do not release the goods to the buyer until your bank has confirmed that the draft is genuine and has been paid.

Paying money into your account

Paying cash into the account

You can pay in cash at your own branch or any other branch of your bank. You need to fill in a paying-in slip – see Chart 2.3. Your bank will normally give you a book of paying-in slips ready printed with your account details and, if you have a cheque book, there will usually be a few paying-in slips printed on the last pages. If you do not have a paying-in slip, ask at the bank counter. Don't forget to fill in the stub or record in your paying-in book, so that you have a note of how much you paid in, when, and where the money came from.

You might also be able to pay in at Post Offices and some cash machines, in which case you'll need special paying-in slips and envelopes provided in advance by your bank. If the cash machine is at a bank branch, there may be a supply of slips and envelopes near the machine.

If you pay in cash at your own branch, you can usually draw out or spend the money straight away. With other methods of paying in, there may be a delay before the money reaches your account – see *Delays before you can draw money out*, on page 34.

Paying in a cheque

You can pay cheques in at any branch of your bank. You may also be able to pay them in at Post Offices and at some cash machines. As with cash (see above), you'll need to fill in a paying-in slip.

There is a delay (generally at least three working days) between paying in a cheque and the money actually being in your account and ready for spending or to withdraw as cash. See *Delays before you can draw money out*, on page 34 for more details.

Example

For his birthday, Rick receives £20 cash from an aunt, a cheque for £50 from his mother and a cheque for £15 from his grandfather. He pays these into his bank account. Chart 2.3 shows how he fills in the paying-in slip.

Chart 2.3 How to fill in a paying-in slip

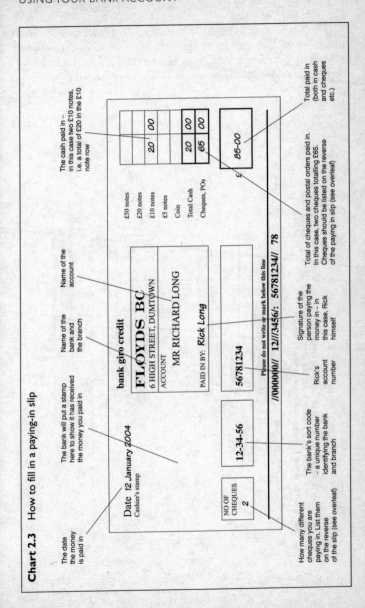

The date the money is paid in

The bank will put a stamp here to show it has received the money you paid in

Name of the bank and the branch

Name of the account

The cash paid in – in this case two £10 notes, i.e. a total of £20 in the £10 note row

Total paid in (both in cash and cheques etc.)

Total of cheques and postal orders paid in. In this case, two cheques totalling £65. Cheques should be listed on the reverse of the paying in slip (see overleaf)

Signature of the person paying the money in – in this case, Rick himself

Rick's account number

The bank's sort code – a unique number identifying the bank and branch

How many different cheques you are paying in. List them on the reverse of the slip (see overleaf)

Within the slip:

Date 12 January 2004
Cashier's stamp

bank giro credit

FLOYDS BC
6 HIGH STREET, DUMTOWN
ACCOUNT
MR RICHARD LONG

PAID IN BY: *Rick Long*

£50 notes	
£20 notes	
£10 notes	20 00
£5 notes	
Coin	
Total Cash	20 00
Cheques, POs	65 00
£	85-00

12-34-56

56781234

NO OF CHEQUES 2

Please do not write or mark below this line

//000000// 12//3456/: 56781234// 78

On the back of the paying-in slip identify each cheque and postal order you are paying in. Usually it is enough to put just the sort code of the bank of the person paying you (which is shown on the cheque)

Put the amount of each cheque or postal order

Add up all the cheques and postal orders. Put the total here and also in the box on the front of the slip (see above)

Cheques, POs

	£	p
65-43-21	50	00
98-76-54	15	00
Total carried over	65	00

Arranging to be paid automatically

You can arrange to have things such as your student loan or wages from a job paid direct to your bank account. To set this up, you give the person paying you the following details:

- the name of your bank
- the name of your branch (usually its address)
- the sort code of your branch
- the name of your account (usually your own name)
- the number of your account.

There will be a delay (usually at least three working days) between money leaving the account of the person paying you and it reaching your account, so you should check that the expected amount has arrived before you start to spend it. An employer will normally arrange for your pay to arrive at your account on a set day each month, although there may be delays because of weekends and bank holidays.

Keeping track of your money

Your bank or building society will send you regular statements listing all the amounts paid into and out of your account and your account balance (i.e., the amount of money left after all the transactions in and out). With some accounts, the norm is one statement every three months, but you can ask for more frequent statements – monthly is a good idea. Some cash machines let you print out a free mini-statement listing your most recent transactions.

Check your statement as soon as you receive it and contact your bank or building society immediately if there is anything wrong – for example, a payment you don't recognise. Match each item on the statement to your debit-card payment slips, cash machine receipts, chequebook and paying-in stubs/records, and so on.

Generally statements show your 'cleared balance', so:

- money paid into your account within the last few days is usually not listed and not yet added to the balance

---

Delays before you can draw money out

When you pay money into your account, there is usually a delay of at least three working days (and often longer) before that money reaches your account and you can use it. This is called the 'clearing' period.

The terms and conditions for the account or other literature that you were given when you opened the account should tell you how long the delay will be.

The clearing period came about originally because when you pay in a cheque, it has physically to be returned to the bank of the person who wrote the cheque (the 'drawer'). That bank checks that there is enough money in the drawer's account, in which case the cheque is paid. If there is not enough money, the cheque is returned to your bank unpaid – in other words the cheque 'bounces'. When money is paid into your account in other ways (for example, cash paid in via a Post Office or wages paid by direct credit), banks still usually insist on a clearing period of a few days even though no physical transfer of paperwork is required. While the money is in limbo between accounts, banks are earning interest on it.

In general, you cannot withdraw money that has not yet cleared. At its discretion your bank might decide to let you draw out uncleared funds, but will usually still charge you if as a result your cleared balance goes into the red and you become overdrawn.

- payments you have made within the last few days are not listed and not yet subtracted from the balance.

However, be aware that sometimes a cheque paid into your account is included in the balance even though there is still some risk that it might bounce. This is because the process of collecting payment from the bank of the person who wrote the cheque sometimes takes longer than the normal clearing period your bank allows. So, if the timing of money coming in and payments you must make is very tight, you might want to phone your bank to check that a payment has really cleared rather than relying on the information in your statement.

CHAPTER 3

Budgeting

Budgeting means managing your spending so that you keep within your income. It is essential if you are living on a tight income, for example as a student. But it's a good habit to get into even if you don't yet have to support yourself. Instead of blowing your allowance or wages each pay day, look ahead and anticipate what you'll need or want to spend over the coming weeks or months.

According to a survey by Nationwide Building Society, one in three 16- to 25-year olds say that managing money is their biggest cause of stress – well ahead of either relationships or jobs.

Drawing up a budget

The step towards gaining control of your money is to draw up a budget. You can use the calculator opposite to help you, or set up something similar as a spreadsheet on your computer.

First, decide whether you want to draw up a weekly or a monthly budget. For many people, monthly will be most appropriate, but, if you are paid weekly, that might be the better basis. To convert amounts from one basis to another:

- **yearly to monthly**; divide by 12
- **yearly to weekly**; divide by 52
- **weekly to monthly**; multiply by 52 and divide by 12
- **monthly to weekly**; multiply by 12 and divide by 52.

Next, look at your sources of income. These might include pocket money or an allowance from parents and other relatives, earnings from a job, student loans, income from savings, and so on. In general, young people tend not to be eligible for state benefits, but you might be in the particular circumstances described on page 40.

On the other side of the equation, tot up your spending. Your bank statements can help you to check this. Alternatively, you could keep a record for a few weeks of everything you spend so that you can see where the money goes – but you need to be honest with yourself because it's surprising how even the tiny sums mount up.

Subtract your spending from your income and what have you got? If the answer is greater than zero, that's fine. You are spending within your means and could even think about saving – see Chapter 7. If it's a negative answer, you have a problem. Your spending exceeds your income. You need urgently to cut back your spending and/or find extra income. If you don't, you risk getting into debt.

Table 3.1 Your budget

Step 1		Your figures
Decide whether to fill in this form with weekly or monthly amounts. Stick to the same basis throughout.		(either per week or per month)

Step 2: Your income

Allowance/pocket money	a1	
Wages/salary (after any deductions for National Insurance, tax, pension etc. – see Chapter 9)	a2	
Student loan – see Chapter 10	a3	
Income from savings	a4	
State benefits – see page 40	a5	
Other	a6	
TOTAL (add up all the amounts a1 to a6)	A	

Step 3: Your spending

Rent or mortgage	b1	
Council tax	b2	
Water rates	b3	
Fuel bills	b4	
Buildings insurance	b5	
Possessions/contents insurance – see Chapter 11	b6	
TV licence	b7	
Housekeeping	b8	
Travelling costs other than car	b9	
Car expenses	b10	
Clothing	b11	
Phone	b12	
Other	b13	
TOTAL (add up all the amounts b1 to b13)	B	

Step 4: Are you living within your income?

Subtract B from A. If the answer is less than zero, you have a problem.	C	

Cutting back on spending

Spending falls into two types:

- **needs** – for example, rent, food, paying bills such as gas and electricity, travel pass and buying basic clothes and footwear
- **wants** – although you might reckon some of these are essential, wants generally include things like nights out, booze

and cigarettes, CDs, videos and DVDs, fashion clothes and running a car if there are public transport alternatives.

If you are spending beyond your means, the first areas to cut back on are your 'wants'. But be realistic. If, say, you know that you'll find it impossible to kick smoking, there's no point planning on saving £4 a day that way. Even when it comes to needs, you may be able to save some money, for example by switching to cheaper purchases. Here are a few ideas that can help you cut your spending.

- Pasta, potatoes and rice are cheap ways to feed yourself, especially if you buy really big packs.
- If you can, shop at discount food stores such as Aldi and Lidl.
- Seek out the special offers (buy one, get one free and bulk buys) in supermarkets. If you can't afford a bulk purchase or wouldn't get through the goods before the use-by date, consider joining forces with a friend and splitting the savings.
- Check whether there is a pick-your-own site or farm shop in your area – they are usually significantly cheaper than buying in supermarkets.
- If you are selective, car-boot sales and table-top sales can be great places to pick up good quality stuff cheaply. Bear in mind that many stallholders are often willing to haggle, especially towards closing time.
- Charity shops can also be a source of bargains and also unusual items that give you scope to create your own individual style.
- Volunteering to help run gigs, film nights, theatre and so on may provide the opportunity to enjoy the entertainment for free. And it's a good way to meet new people.
- If you are renting, maybe you could squeeze in an extra housemate to spread the rent and other costs a bit further.
- Shop around for your gas and electricity suppliers. According to the consumer watchdog, Energywatch, this could save you as much as £100 a year. To compare suppliers and for advice on making a switch, visit the Energywatch★ or Switch with Which?★ websites.

- Arrange to pay fuel and phone bills by direct debit – you usually get a small discount.
- Use less fuel by switching off unnecessary lights, using energy-efficient light bulbs, stopping draughts, closing curtains at night, putting the plug in the basin or sink when you run hot water, and turning down your heating a little (a 1°C reduction could knock a tenth off your bills). For more tips, see *www.saveenergy.co.uk*.
- Check whether you're eligible for discounts because you are a school or college student when you shop or at local sports facilities. See if there are other discount schemes running in your area, for example Young Scot★ if you live in Scotland.
- If you need a lift (or have a car and would be willing to offer lifts) – say, to a music festival, sporting event or tourist attraction – consider joining a car-sharing★ scheme.
- Cars are inefficient for short journeys because the engine is cold and a high proportion of the total time may be spent manoeuvring in and out of parking spaces, so try to walk or cycle instead.
- The way you drive can affect the amount of fuel used by as much as 15 per cent. As far as possible, keep to the efficient speed band for your car (usually between 15 and 70mph), minimise stopping (for example, by anticipating traffic lights) and avoid racing starts.

Don't be tempted to cut your spending by breaking the law. If you run a car, you must have car insurance. If you have a TV, you must have a licence. You'll end up paying much more – both in money and other ways – if you are caught.

Spread the load

Paying by instalments can make it easier to manage large bills, and arranging to pay by direct debit means that the instalments are automatically paid on time provided the money is in your bank account.

Boost your income

Tax

Make sure you are not paying tax unnecessarily. Everyone has a personal allowance of a certain amount of income tax-free each year (£4,745 in the 2004–5 tax year). So, if your income is no more than that amount, you should not be paying tax on your earnings or savings income. See Chapters 7 ('Savings and investments') and 9 ('Understanding your pay slip') for guidance on how to check your tax position and claim back any tax incorrectly paid.

State benefits

Check whether you are eligible to claim any state benefits. State benefits are a financial safety net for people who are finding it hard to support themselves. In general, you must be aged 16 and over to be eligible to claim benefits in your own right, because below that age an adult is expected to be financially responsible for you. Many benefits for people of working age (16 up to state pension age) are payable only if you are actually available for work, therefore very few students are eligible to claim benefits. The main exceptions are where you have a child or are disabled.

Most state benefits are either means-tested or contributory. With means-tested benefits, you can qualify only if your income and savings are low. With contributory benefits, you must have paid or been credited with a certain number of National Insurance contributions in order to qualify. You come within the National Insurance system only from age 16 and you'll usually have to work for at least two years before you have built up enough contributions to qualify for any contributory state benefits.

The table below outlines the main state benefits. The benefit system is complicated so, if you think you might qualify, get advice, for example from your local social security office★, your local Citizens Advice Bureau★ or your student union★ welfare office.

Table 3.2 The main state benefits

Name of benefit	Contributory or means-tested	Who it is intended for
Jobseeker's Allowance – contributory	Contributory	Unemployed, available for work
Jobseeker's Allowance – income-related	Means-tested	Unemployed, available for work
Income Support	Means-tested	Low income and savings, not available for work
Housing Benefit	Means-tested	Low income and savings, meets rent costs
Council Tax Benefit	Means-tested	Low income and savings, meets council tax bill
Incapacity Benefit	Contributory	Too ill to work
Disability Living Allowance	Neither	Long-term ill or disabled
Child Benefit	Neither	Supporting a child
Child Tax Credit	Means-tested	Supporting a child
Care to Learn scheme	Neither	Parents aged 16–19 wanting to return to school – meets childcare costs
Working Tax Credit	Means-tested	Working but on a low income

Extra work

Could you boost your income by taking on extra work, either in a current job or by taking a second job? Do you have skills or hobbies that could generate some cash? Even if your time is limited – say, because of school – could you maybe offer coaching to younger pupils during your lunch break?

Rent a room

If you are living in a home that you own or perhaps your parents are providing for you, consider taking in a lodger. The Rent-a-Room Scheme allows you to earn up to £4,250 a year in rents tax-free. For information, see booklet IR87 *Letting and your home* from the Inland Revenue★. If the home is being bought with a mortgage, you'll usually need permission from the lender before taking in tenants.

CHAPTER 4

Borrowing

Borrowing lets you buy things now instead of waiting until you've saved up enough. When you borrow, you enter into a legal agreement – a contract:

- the lender agrees to give you money now
- you often agree to repay the money in regular instalments (usually monthly); some types of borrowing have more flexible repayment arrangements
- in addition, you agree to pay the lender interest. Interest is the price you pay for the loan. There may be other charges as well, such as an arrangement fee when you first take out the loan.

In general, no one will be willing to lend you money while you are under the age of 18. This is because most types of contract can't be enforced against 'minors'. So a lender would not be able to demand its money back!

What you pay to borrow

Borrowing is in most cases an expensive way of buying something compared with saving up and getting it later on. Sometimes, you must have an item now and have no choice but to borrow, but often you do have a choice and should therefore be aware of how much extra you'll have to pay if you decide to borrow – see the table on page 44. Are you sure you want to pay the extra?

The cost of borrowing

If you want to know the cost of most types of borrowing, look for the 'annual percentage rate' (APR). The APR is a way of expressing the interest and any other compulsory charges (such as an arrangement fee or annual fee) in a standardised way. You don't need to know how the APR is worked out. Just be aware that borrowing at a low APR is generally cheaper than borrowing at a higher APR. For example, a personal loan with, say, a 14 per cent APR would be a cheaper type of borrowing than a credit card with an 18 per cent APR.

But cheapness is not everything. Also check out the monthly repayments you'd have to make. Even if the APR says a loan is good value, the cash you have to fork out each month might still be more than you can afford.

The cost of overdrafts is given as an equivalent annual rate (EAR), which includes interest but not any other charges you might incur and so is not directly comparable with an APR.

Table 4.1 How much extra you would pay for an item costing £100 if you borrowed to buy it

The yearly interest rate (APR) on the loan	The extra you would pay if you took this long to pay off the loan:					
	6 months	1 year	2 years	3 years	4 years	5 years
8%	£2	£4	£8	£12	£17	£21
9%	£3	£5	£9	£14	£19	£24
10%	£3	£5	£10	£15	£21	£26
11%	£3	£6	£11	£17	£23	£29
12%	£3	£6	£12	£19	£25	£32
13%	£4	£7	£13	£20	£27	£34
14%	£4	£7	£14	£22	£29	£37
15%	£4	£8	£15	£23	£31	£40
16%	£4	£8	£16	£25	£33	£43
17%	£5	£9	£17	£26	£36	£45
18%	£5	£9	£18	£28	£38	£48
19%	£5	£10	£19	£29	£40	£51
20%	£5	£10	£20	£31	£42	£54
21%	£6	£11	£21	£32	£44	£56
22%	£6	£11	£22	£34	£46	£59
23%	£6	£12	£23	£35	£48	£62
24%	£6	£12	£24	£37	£50	£65
25%	£7	£13	£25	£38	£53	£68
26%	£7	£13	£26	£40	£55	£70
27%	£7	£14	£27	£42	£57	£73
28%	£7	£14	£28	£43	£59	£76
29%	£8	£14	£29	£45	£61	£79
30%	£8	£15	£30	£46	£63	£82

Example

Anna sees a great jacket in the sales and buys some trousers and boots as well. They come to £200 altogether and she pays with her store card (see page 46). She pays off the card balance in equal amounts spread over a year. The interest rate is 26 per cent a year. Table 4.1 tells Anna that she will pay £13 extra for each £100 she borrows compared with buying the clothes without a loan. So the cost of borrowing the £200 is 2 × £13 = £26. In other words, she pays £226 in total for the clothes. Were they such a bargain after all?

Different ways to borrow

Bank overdraft

If you have a current account (see Chapter 1), you may borrow by spending more money than you have in your account. The excess you've spent is called an overdraft.

Some accounts automatically include a small, free overdraft of usually £10 to £50. Student accounts sometimes have a larger free amount. But, in general, the bank will charge for an overdraft.

If you arrange the overdraft with your bank manager in advance, you'll usually pay interest and, with some banks, an arrangement fee. Usually you agree the length of time for which you'll have the overdraft, but it's up to you, within that period, how and when you pay it off. So arranged overdrafts tend to be a cheap and flexible way to borrow. To arrange an overdraft, phone or visit your bank.

The picture is quite different if you go overdrawn without arranging it first. The interest rate is usually much higher and you'll incur extra charges, such as a monthly fee and administration charges for bouncing cheques, the bank writing to you, and so on. If – as is likely – your bank stops payments out of your account, there will be all sorts of knock-on problems to sort out and possibly damage to your credit record (see page 48). Avoid unarranged overdrafts like the plague.

According to a survey for Nationwide Building Society, seven out of ten people in the UK have an overdraft. One in five people who do not have an arranged overdraft facility admit to slipping into the red.

Personal loan

If you want to buy something big, such as a car, a personal loan may be suitable. You borrow a lump sum and agree to pay it back in set monthly instalments over a fixed period. Typically, the interest rate is fixed for the duration of the loan, so your monthly payments do not vary. If you want to pay off the loan early, there is usually an early repayment charge.

Many people approach their usual bank to ask for a personal loan or sometimes the shop or salesperson selling the goods can arrange the loan for you, but you can go to any other lender and will often pay less by shopping around. The personal finance sections of national newspapers usually carry a table summarising best-buy loans, and comparisons are also available from Moneyfacts★ and many personal finance websites, such as FTYourMoney★ and MoneySupermarket★.

Credit cards

You borrow by using the card to pay for goods and services (or to draw money from cash machines). Whatever you borrow is billed to your credit-card account and, once a month, you pay off at least a minimum amount. You choose when to pay off the rest of the balance. If you pay off the whole lot each month, there is usually no interest to pay, in which case this is a cheap, flexible way to borrow for a short period. If you don't pay off the full balance, there is interest to pay. For more about credit cards, see Chapter 5.

Store cards

Most store cards work like credit cards (see above), except that you can use them to pay for things only in particular shops.

A few store cards are budget cards. With these, you agree to pay a set amount each month, say, from £5 to £30. You can then, depending on the card, borrow 20, 24 or 30 times the amount of the monthly payment. So, for example, if you agree to pay £20 a month, you might be allowed to borrow up to 30 x £20 = £600 in total.

As a store cardholder, you may be eligible for special perks, such as discounts and sale previews. But you generally pay for these privileges because most store cards charge a very high rate of interest. This makes store cards one of the most expensive ways to borrow and they are best avoided altogether.

Borrowing wisely

- Consider saving up to buy later instead of borrowing to buy now. You not only save the cost of borrowing, but your savings also earn interest – see Chapter 7.
- Decide what sort of borrowing would suit you best, given the length of time for which you want to borrow and the cost.
- Borrow only if you have worked out in advance how to pay off the money.
- Borrow only if you are sure you can manage the repayments within your budget – see Chapter 3.
- Shop around for a competitive deal. Compare APRs to decide which deal is cheapest. But check for additional charges.
- Read the contract before you sign up. Make sure you understand what happens if, say, you want to pay off the loan early or you run into problems making the repayments.
- If you run into problems making repayments, don't bury your head in the sand. Debt problems do not go away – they just get worse.
- If your debts get out of hand, get help – see Chapter 6.

Other shop credit

Sometimes you are offered interest-free credit – especially when buying electrical goods, such as a hi-fi, TV or fridge. Check out the deal carefully. The credit may be free, but could you buy the goods cheaper elsewhere? How long is the interest-free period and what happens at the end of it? Often the interest-free credit is conditional on your paying in full at the end of the period. If you don't, interest is charged and backdated to the date of purchase.

Catalogue shopping

Shopping from a mail-order catalogue can seem attractive if you're on a tight budget because you can usually spread the payments over a large number of small instalments. That helps your cash flow, but can work out expensive in the long run with you paying much more than the cash price. Also check that the catalogue prices are competitive – you may be able to buy cheaper on the high street.

Student loans

For details of these, see Chapter 10.

Table 4.2 Cost of different types of borrowing

Type of borrowing	Typical cost
Arranged overdraft	6.75% to 18.9% (EAR)
Personal loan	6.7% to 20.9% (APR)
Credit card	7.8% to 24.9% (APR)
Store card	13% to 30.9% (APR)
Unauthorised overdraft	14.4% to 41.2% (EAR)

Source: Moneyfacts, October 2003.

Secured loans

A secured loan is a loan taken out against some valuable item, most often your home if you own it. Secured loans are cheaper than other types of borrowing because the lender is taking less risk. If you fail to keep up the repayments, the lender can sell the valuable item and take what is owed from the proceeds. By the same token, a secured loan is more risky for you because you stand to lose the item.

Are you creditworthy?

In broad terms, an ideal customer from a lender's point of view is someone who borrows a lot, always makes his or her repayments on time and preferably does not pay off the loan early. If there's a risk that you might not keep up the repayments, a lender may still lend to you but will generally want to charge a higher rate of interest to compensate for that risk. So, before deciding to lend, companies try to assess what sort of customer you will be.

To do this, they often carry out a credit-scoring exercise. This involves asking you various questions which will be on the form you fill in when you apply for a card or loan. You are given points for each answer. The loan will be offered to you only if your points add up to at least a pre-set score. Each company has its own credit-scoring method, which is usually a closely guarded secret, but the sort of things it will be interested in include where you live, your employment status, your income, whether you are a homeowner, whether you have a bank account, what other debts you already have, and so on.

Companies will also check out your file with one or more credit-reference agencies. Just about every adult in the UK has such a file, but if you are in your late teens or early twenties, there might not be much recorded on it. The file contains public information including your name and address taken from the electoral register. Your credit file also includes information about existing loans and credit that you have, together with a record of whether or not you have been making the repayments as agreed and on time. It also records each time a credit check is made against your file.

Your credit file includes information about you and anyone living at the same address with whom you have a financial connection. It's generally assumed that someone is connected to you if they share your surname or have taken out a loan jointly with you.

Refused credit?

Different lenders specialise in different types of business, so being turned down for credit by one lender does not necessarily mean there is anything wrong or that you will be turned down by others.

On the other hand, mistakes do happen and you might be wrongly refused credit because of an error on your credit file. If a lender turns you down, you have the right to know whether the lender consulted a credit-reference agency and, if so, which one. It could be worth checking the file. Common mistakes include:

CHAPTER 5

Plastic fantastic?

Come your eighteenth birthday, credit-card companies will fall over themselves to sign you up and you may be very tempted by all that lovely new spending power. However, heed the words of an expert – Matt Barrett, boss of Barclays (the largest credit-card lender in Europe) is on record as saying: 'I don't borrow on credit cards because it's too expensive.' In practice, credit cards can be useful, but only if you are very disciplined and handle them sensibly.

What is a credit card?

A credit card is a flexible way to borrow. You can use the card to pay for goods and services (and draw cash from cash machines, though this is expensive and not recommended – see page 56).

Each time you use the card, the amount spent is added to your account. The balance on the account is the amount you have borrowed. The card issuer sets you an upper credit limit (usually at least £500) and, provided you don't exceed that limit, it's up to you how much you borrow, when and for how long.

Credit cards are issued by banks, though often they are branded with another organisation's name. Most cards are in either the Visa or MasterCard network (these organisations sort out which outlets accept their cards and settle all the transactions).

How does a credit card work?

The physical process of using a credit card to buy something or draw out cash from a machine is the same as already described for debit cards in Chapter 2. However, there the similarity ends.

With a credit card, you get a statement each month listing every transaction you've made and showing the balance of your account – see Chart 5.1 opposite. You are required to pay off at least a minimum sum each month. The amount varies, but is typically 3 per cent of the account balance or £5, whichever is higher. You can choose to pay off more.

Unless you pay off the whole of the outstanding balance, you are charged interest on the items shown on the statement including any balance carried over from the previous month. The interest is added to the following month's statement.

If you pay off the balance in full, usually no interest is added to your account the following month, so you have an interest-free loan from the time you make each purchase up to the date you pay off the bill in full. However, there will usually still be some interest to pay if you have used your card to draw out cash.

In addition to charging you interest, card issuers make money by charging retailers a fee each time they accept payment by credit card. Small retailers sometimes pass on this fee by charging you more if you pay by credit card rather than cash. Larger retailers usually charge the same price however you choose to pay.

Example

Julie gets a credit-card statement. It says she must pay off at least £7.04 this month. This is 3 per cent of the balance of £234.58. See Chart 5.1 opposite.

Chart 5.1 A credit-card statement

Julie paid off her last bill in full

FLOYDCARD

Card reference: 1234 4321 5678 8765

Customer services: 0870 000 0 000   www.floydcard.co.uk

Account holder: Ms Julie Sweets

Account details

Date	Transaction	Amount
12 Dec	BHS, Dumtown	£52.96
17 Dec	Boots, Dumtown	£21.98
17 Dec	Ottakar's, Dumtown	£10.00
17 Dec	W H Smith, Dumtown	£62.87
23 Dec	Tesco store 0123, Dumtown	£78.06
2 Jan	Safeway, Dumtown	£8.71
8 Jan	Interest charge 8 January	£0.00
8 Jan	**New balance**	**£234.58**

Because Julie paid off her last bill in full, no interest is added to this statement

Account summary

On 8 January 2004	
Previous balance	£32.02
Payments received	£32.02
New transactions	£234.58
New balance	£234.58

The bill this month is £234.58. Julie must pay off at least £7.04 by 3 February

Payment due

Minimum payment	£7.04
Payment date	3 February 2004
Purchase APR	15.9%
Cash APR	18.3%
Next month's estimated interest	£5.11

If Julie does not pay off the bill in full, she will be charged interest on the purchases she has made this month at this rate of interest

Credit limit

Current limit	£1,000.00
Available credit	£705.42
(this may reflect recent transactions not included on this statement)	

If Julie paid off just the minimum payment (£7.04 this time), the card company estimates that she will have to pay £5.11 in interest on the items that appear on this statement. The £5.11 would be added to her next statement

What do credit cards cost?

Credit cards have a reputation for being a particularly expensive way to borrow, but this depends on the card you choose and how you use it.

The card you choose

In October 2003, the standard interest rate on credit cards ranged from 8 per cent up to 25 per cent, depending on the card. Many store cards cost even more. So picking the wrong card can be an expensive mistake.

However, the cheapest cards are often offered by companies who decide what to charge you based on your credit standing. This is assessed mainly by looking at your financial history – see Chapter 4. If you are young, you will not usually have had time to build up much financial history, so you might not be eligible for the very cheapest rates. Even so, there is no reason for you to put up with a card charging 25 per cent – shop around.

Some cards offer low introductory interest rates – even 0 per cent – for a limited period. These can be a good deal, but check that the rate you'll pay once the introductory period (typically six months) has ended is also competitive. If not, be prepared to switch cards again once the introductory period is up.

If you already have a card, you might be tempted by invitations to transfer your outstanding balance to a new card offering a low, or even zero, rate on balance transfers for a period of, say, six months. This might be worth doing, but check the detail of the scheme. Typically, if you also use the new card to make fresh purchases, you will find that your repayments are set first against the transferred balance not the new purchases. This means the transferred balance may be paid off early and you end up paying more interest than you'd expected. A way around this is to switch your balance to a card with a good deal on transfers but use another card to make any new purchases.

Example

Rick has run up £500 on his CostuCard and is paying around £17 a month in interest. He sees that a rival card, Comonova, is offering 0 per cent interest for six months on balance transfers. Making the switch should save him 6 × £17 = £102. Rick then uses the card to pay £300 for a new hi-fi system. But, although he pays off the £300 at the next statement date, he is shocked to see he has started to pay interest again even though the six-month transfer deal period is not up. This happens because the £300 repayment is set first against the £500 balance transfer, leaving only £200 to benefit from the 0 per cent interest deal. The remaining £300 is charged at the card's standard interest rate.

How you use your card

Usually, if you pay off your credit card bill in full each month, you do not pay interest. Used this way, a credit card is not so much a form of borrowing but more a convenient way to pay for things. Of course, you'd get the same convenience by using a debit card (see Chapter 2), but a credit card has a couple of advantages:

- you get an interest-free loan from the date of the purchase up to the date you pay off the card balance. This could be handy if, say, you are waiting for your wages to go into the bank
- for a purchase costing more than £100, you get extra protection when you use a credit card under section 75 of the Consumer Credit Act 1974. This says that, if there is a problem with the goods or services you've bought, then the card company is responsible as well as the retailer. So, for example, if you paid for a holiday with your card and the tour operator went bust, you could claim a refund from the card company.

If you don't pay off your balance in full each month, you will be charged interest. Unless you have an expensive card, this can still work out as a fairly economical way to borrow for up to a few months. However, if you borrow for longer it is usually cheaper to arrange an overdraft with your bank.

Using credit cards to draw out cash

You can use your credit card in a cash machine to draw out cash, but usually this is not a good idea because:

- there is nearly always a handling fee, say 2 per cent of the amount you draw out or £2, whichever is more
- even if you pay off your bill in full, you will usually have to pay interest from the date the cash is drawn out up to either the statement date or the date you pay off the bill
- the interest rate charged on cash withdrawals is higher than the standard rate charged on purchases.

So, being able to draw cash is a useful back-up in an emergency, but expensive if you make a habit of it.

If you use your card to pay for foreign currency, for example at your bank or a bureau de change, this will be treated as a cash withdrawal and charged accordingly.

Using credit cards abroad

Chapter 13 looks in detail at the different ways to sort out your holiday money, including using your credit card in many places abroad. As far as cost goes, the transaction will be converted from the foreign currency into pounds on the date it reaches your account (not the date you spent the money). Although the exchange rate used is often competitive (because your card company will be exchanging currencies in bulk), most card companies add an extra charge called an 'exchange rate loading', which is typically 1.75 to 2.75 per cent of the amount of the transaction.

Other charges

A few cards charge an annual fee, usually £10 or £20, but with so many alternative cards to choose from, it's easy to avoid this.

If you fail to make the minimum monthly repayment or send it in after the due date, there will usually be a late payment fee of, say, £15 or £20. A similar charge is likely to be made if you exceed your credit limit.

Donation cards

Some credit cards are associated with charities. When you take up one of these cards, each time you use it the card issuer makes a donation to the charity. Typically, this might be £10 when you first get the card and then 0.25 per cent of anything you subsequently spend on it.

These cards are worthwhile only if you were already in the market for a credit card and the terms of the card (including the interest rate) are suitable for you. If not, you'd do better to shop around for a more suitable credit card and separately make donations to charity.

Choosing a credit card

Before choosing a card, you should be sure that you really want one.

Do you need a credit card?

Very few people actually *need* a credit card. Table 5.1 sets out the pros and cons which may help you to decide whether you *want* one. Before deciding, be honest with yourself – if you are an impulsive person who finds it hard to keep to a budget, you are probably safer avoiding credit cards altogether. Only consider a card if you are confident you have the self-discipline to keep your spending under control. See Chapter 3 for guidance on living on a budget and Chapter 6 for what to do if debts get on top of you.

How to shop around

Once you reach 18, you'll probably get a lot of junk mail offering you credit cards, but these may not be the best on offer so it's a good idea to do your own homework. The easiest way to compare credit-card deals is to go onto the Internet and visit one of the many personal finance sites, such as FTYourMoney★ or MoneySupermarket★. The definitive provider of this sort of information is Moneyfacts★. You'll find its comparisons published in the personal finance sections of newspapers and in personal finance magazines, but they are also available direct from Moneyfacts via its website, by fax or in its monthly magazine, which you may be able to find in larger reference libraries.

Table 5.1 Pros and cons of credit cards

Pros	Cons
Flexible, for example lets you easily take advantage of an unexpected deal	May encourage you to buy things you can't really afford
Convenient way to pay for things, especially large items	You can quickly build up large debts
Free short-term credit provided you pay off your bill in full each month	Expensive way to borrow if you don't pay off your balance within a few months
Lets you buy something now but put off paying for a short while until some expected money comes in	Risk that you will run up large debts with no idea of how to pay them off
Extra protection when you buy something costing more than £100 because you can claim against the card company or the retailer	

What to look for

This depends on how you will use the card. If you expect to pay off the bill in full each month, the interest rate will be largely irrelevant. Instead, you might look at the length of the interest-free period and what extras, if any, the card offers. For example, some cards offer points that you can 'spend' on a range of goods and services or AirMiles. But usually you have to use the card an awful lot before you clock up enough points to be worth having. Research by *Which?* suggests that the only really worthwhile perk is cashback, where you get a refund in cash according to how much you spend on your card. Table 5.2 shows the cards that were offering cashbacks in October 2003.

If you are unlikely to pay off your bill in full every month, go for a card with a low interest rate – as measured by the annual percentage rate (APR) described in Chapter 4.

From the end of March 2004, card companies are committed to including a summary box on all application forms and promotional material such as mailshots. The summary box will present the key features of a card in a format that will help you to compare one card with another more easily. The features in the box include:

- APRs and the monthly interest rates
- the interest-free period (if you pay off your balance in full)
- how your payments are allocated to your outstanding and any transferred balance
- the minimum monthly repayment
- fees and charges.

Table 5.2 Credit cards offering cashback deals

Card issuer	Type of card
Abbey National	Cashback MasterCard or Visa
Alliance & Leicester	Moneyback MasterCard or Visa
American Express	Blue Amex
Bank of Ireland	Moneyback MasterCard
Birmingham Midshires	Classic Cashback Visa
Circle Rebate	MasterCard
Egg	Visa
First Trust Bank	Visa Option 1
Halifax	Classic Cashback MasterCard or Visa
Leeds & Holbeck	MasterCard
Morgan Stanley	Cashback MasterCard
Nationwide	Cash Reward Visa
RAC	Visa
Smile	Visa

Source: Moneyfacts, October 2003.

How to apply for a credit card

Once you have decided on the card you want, phone the card company for an application form. If it is an Internet-based card, you can usually apply online, though a copy of the agreement will be posted to you for signing.

If your application is accepted, you will be sent a card. Sign the back of it straight away. Separately (for security reasons), you will be sent a PIN to use with the card. See Chapter 2 for more about PINs.

Credit-card fraud

In 2002, £425 million was lost through credit-card fraud. A third of this was due to counterfeiting, where criminals use real card details on a fake card. The most common way they get hold of the card details is through 'skimming'. This happens when you hand over your card to pay for something – typically in a bar, restaurant or garage. The card will be taken out of your view – perhaps only for seconds – and, as well as processing the genuine transaction, a corrupt employee quickly passes your card through a machine that can read and copy the details on your card's magnetic strip. These are transferred to the counterfeit card and the criminals then go shopping at your expense. The first you know something is wrong is usually when you get your statement showing purchases you haven't made.

To fight this type of fraud, card companies are now phasing out cards with a magnetic strip and replacing them with 'chip and PIN' cards. The information encoded on the card is stored on a microchip, making the cards much more difficult to copy. The aim is to replace all current UK credit and debit cards with this kind of card by 2005.

You can guard against fraud by:

- looking after your card as carefully as you would cash
- not letting your card out of your sight when paying
- being careful when throwing away credit-card slips and old statements – if possible, shred them so no one can piece together your financial details
- checking your statements carefully and alerting your card company immediately if you spot any rogue transactions
- keeping your PIN safe (see page 23)
- using your card over the phone or online only if you are sure you are dealing with a genuine, reputable firm. Never give your card details to a cold caller.

Your rights as a credit-card customer

Credit cards are covered by the Consumer Credit Act 1974 which gives card users various rights. In particular, if your card is lost or stolen and misused by criminals, the maximum loss you will have to bear is £50. This protection applies even if you have not taken reasonable care, for example, to keep your PIN safe. This is different from the protection applying in the case of debit cards, where you could be liable for the full loss if you have not acted with reasonable care, though it would be for the bank to prove this was the case. In practice, most card issuers will let you off even the first £50 of losses.

Under the Act, if your card details are misused while the card is still in your possession, you are not responsible for any losses. Similarly, you can't be held liable if a new or replacement card is intercepted and misused before it even reaches you.

Under European legislation, when you buy something at a distance – for example, by phone or Internet – using a credit (or debit) card, you cannot be held liable for any loss due to unauthorised use of your card details, for example by hackers.

Hacker at the gates

To demonstrate the inadequacy of online security, 19-year-old Raphael Gray hacked into company websites and posted 23,000 stolen credit-card details on the Internet. Finding the card details of Microsoft's founder among them, Raphael used the information to order a course of Viagra, billed and delivered to Bill Gates.

CHAPTER 6

Coping with debt

Reaching the age of 18 may open the door to credit, but it also opens it to potential debt problems. It may seem strange to warn about the dangers of debt when students are being encouraged to go to university and in the process run up debts of tens of thousands of pounds in student loans and fees. But the problem with any debt is not so much the amount that is borrowed, but whether you have a manageable plan for repayment. One of the biggest dangers whatever your age is letting credit-card spending run away with you. It is all too easy to spend, spend, spend, while paying off just the minimum each month, which can easily result in a card bill of thousands and no way to pay it off.

Managing student loans and top-up fees is considered in Chapter 10. Here, we look at coping with other types of debt if they get out of hand.

The warning signs

You may have a debt problem if any of these apply:

- you are running up an overdraft or credit-card debt just to pay for essential spending on, for example, food or rent
- you pay off just the minimum on credit- or store-card bills each month and would find it hard to pay off any extra
- you are taking out new loans or credit in order to pay off existing debts
- you have given up opening your post because you can't face more bills
- you are already behind with one or more loan or credit repayment
- you are behind with your rent or fuel bills or, if you have one, your mortgage.

> Don't ignore growing debts – tackle them sooner rather than later.

What happens if you run up debts?

If you miss the odd credit- or store-card repayment, not much will happen. There will usually be a penalty charge and, of course, your debt won't have got any smaller. But if you persistently miss credit-card repayments, you will soon run into more serious problems. The same is true of missed loan repayments and unpaid bills for fuel and rent. The precise consequences depend on the type of debt concerned.

Some debts are 'priority debts'. This means that the person to whom you owe money (the 'creditor') has the legal right to take serious steps to recover his or her money. Table 6.1 summarises the action that can be taken against you if you don't pay priority debts.

Table 6.1 What can happen if you don't pay priority debts

Type of debt problem	What can happen
You fail to pay rent	You could be evicted
You don't keep up mortgage repayments	The lender can take your home away from you
You don't pay fuel bills	Your gas or electricity can be cut off
You don't pay your phone bill	The phone can be cut off (not a priority debt if you could manage without a phone)
You don't pay your TV licence	You can be fined and/or sent to jail and your possessions can be seized to pay the arrears and fines
You don't pay your council tax	You can be fined and/or sent to jail and your possessions can be seized to pay the arrears and fines
You don't pay other taxes	You can be fined, your possessions can be seized to pay the arrears and fines; you could be declared bankrupt
You don't pay magistrates' court fines	You can be sent to jail and/or your possessions can be seized to pay the arrears
You don't keep up hire-purchase payments (e.g. for a car)	The lender can take back the goods (only a priority debt if the goods are essential – e.g. you need a car to get to work)

Other types of debt are usually non-priority debts, because all the lender can do is take you to court. The court will assess what you need to live on and usually order that any surplus is divided between your creditors to pay off gradually all that you owe. This arrangement is called a 'county court judgment' or CCJ.

If your debts are very severe, you may be declared bankrupt. In that case, things you own are sold and, for a time – usually one year (three years before 1 April 2004) – trustees control your money to ensure that your creditors get back as much as possible of the money they are owed. However, you will be allowed to keep possessions that are considered necessities, such as clothes and basic household equipment.

Having a CCJ or being declared bankrupt will affect your creditworthiness (see Chapter 4), and make it harder in future for you to get normal credit – for example, a credit card, mortgage or other loan, or quarterly bill arrangement for the phone or fuel (since this involves credit because you use the service in advance of paying). Some lenders will still lend to you if you have a bad credit record, but you have to pay a much higher interest rate and often a hefty arrangement fee, which may just exacerbate your debt problems.

ONE OF THE BIGGEST DANGERS IS LETTING CREDIT CARD SPENDING RUN AWAY WITH YOU.

What to do if you have a debt problem

The most important step is to admit that you have a problem. The longer you deny the problem, the worse it will become and the more difficult it will be to sort out.

Once you've recognised the problem, here are the steps you should take.

Step 1 Don't borrow any more – for example, cut up your credit and store cards, and if you have a full current account, switch instead to a basic bank account that does not let you run up an overdraft.

Step 2 Work out your budget (in other words, what you have coming in each week or month and what you spend). Cut out all unnecessary spending. Can you increase your income, for example by working more hours or claiming state benefits? Work out how much you can afford each week or month to pay off your debts.

Step 3 Prioritise your debts – see page 64. You'll need to concentrate on paying off priority debts first. Anything left over can be put towards clearing the non-priority debts. Allocate money to non-priority debts according to the amount you owe. For example, if you have one debt of £1,000 and another of £2,000, put one-third of the money towards paying off the first debt and two-thirds towards paying off the second.

Step 4 Contact your creditors straight away. To each one, explain the problem and how you intend to pay off your debt. With non-priority creditors, offer to pay off the debt bit by bit, even if it's only £1 a week. Most creditors know this is exactly what a court would order, so they have little to gain by taking you to court. Deal with your creditors in writing. That way, you're less likely to be pressurised into agreeing to higher payments than you can afford. You'll also have a record of what has been agreed. If you do deal by phone or face to face, take notes of what has been said and agreed.

Step 5 If you owe money to the bank that operates your main account, you will probably need to open a new account. If not, the bank will automatically set money coming into your account against what you owe the bank, leaving you unable to implement your plans to repay other creditors. In the past, it was well nigh impossible to open a new bank account if you already had a debt problem. However, these days, the major banks all offer basic bank accounts (see Chapter 1), most of which are available even if your credit standing is not good.

Don't struggle alone. There are lots of organisations that can help you to sort out debt problems – see overleaf.

Drawing up a budget

Be realistic about the money you will need to cover essential spending such as on food and clothing; otherwise, you risk calculating debt repayments that you can't maintain.

Debt consolidation

You may be tempted by the adverts of debt-consolidation companies. These companies offer to replace all your existing loans with a single ('consolidated') loan, so that only one loan repayment is required each month. Your monthly outlay should fall, normally because the new loan is secured (see below), or because you contract to repay it over a longer period than the loans being replaced.

Consolidating your debts could be a good idea, although you don't necessarily need the help of a debt-consolidation company, which will of course charge a fee for its services. There's nothing to stop you shopping around for a better-value loan and using it to pay off more expensive debts. For example, you might take out a personal loan from a bank (with structured repayments over a fixed number of years) as a way of paying off more expensive credit- and store-card loans.

Debt-consolidation companies often target only homeowners. This is because the consolidated loan can then be secured against the home, making it less risky for the lender and cheaper for the borrower. But you then stand to lose your home if you fail to keep up the repayments on the consolidated loan, so you should think twice before going down this route.

Whatever you do, don't consolidate all your debts and then use the money saved each month as an excuse to finance new debts. Your debt problems will just get worse.

Don't feel guilty about debt

You've done nothing wrong. You've simply got into difficulties like thousands of other people every day.

Who to contact if you have a debt problem

The following organisations offer free help and advice with debt problems, or can put you in touch with other bodies that do. If you are a student, your student union will usually be able to put you in touch with a money adviser. Help may include, for example, working out a budget, negotiating with creditors, and assisting with state benefits claims.

- Citizens Advice Bureau★
- National Debtline★
- Community Legal Service★
- Consumer Credit Counselling Service (CCCS)★.

Who not to contact

You'd think that commercial businesses would not be interested in you when you have no money. Think again! There are all sorts of companies out there which have devised ways to profit from your debts.

Debt-management companies do not make loans, but offer to act as a bridge between you and your creditors. You pay a single monthly sum to the debt-management company, which then passes on part to each creditor, having negotiated with the creditor on your behalf. Sounds good, but unfortunately these companies have developed a reputation for bad service and high charges. Often, they fail to negotiate with all your creditors, ignoring the all-important priority debts. Typically, the whole of your first month's payment will be taken in fees and also, say, 15 per cent of each subsequent payment. To crown it all, you do not need the help of these companies because you can get debt advice and help completely free from the organisations listed above.

Once you have had debt problems, you are likely to have a poor credit record, with the result that you will be turned down for credit or be charged extra. Credit-repair agencies offer – for a fee – to clean up your credit record. Again, you do not need these companies. Anything legal that they can do for you, you can easily do for yourself. Chapter 4 explains how you can get a copy of your record from a credit-reference agency for just £2 a time; the information you get back will tell you what to do to correct any error on your file. There is no legal way to erase correct information from your file.

Example

Sean is 20 and works as an electronics technician. He earns £183 a week. He shares a two-bedroomed terraced house with a friend and they split the household bills between them. Luckily, he lives within walking distance of work, so does not need a car. Even so, for some time Sean has been having problems making ends meet. Now his bank has written to say that it has declined to pay the direct debit Sean set up for his share of the rent because his bank account is overdrawn. Sean turns to his local money advice centre for help. They take him through the following steps.

1 Stop borrowing Sean stops non-essential spending and cuts up his credit card to remove temptation.

2 Draw up a budget Sean's weekly income and outgoings are as shown in Table 6.2. By cutting down on his non-essential spending, Sean reckons he can set aside nearly £27 a week for paying off the debts.

Table 6.2 Sean's weekly budget

Item	What Sean has been spending	What Sean plans to spend in future
Income		
Earnings after deducting tax and National Insurance	£183.20	£183.20
Spending		
Rent	£49.62	£49.62
Phone	£5.00	£0.00
Electricity and gas	£3.85	£3.85
Water rates	£2.40	£2.40
Council tax	£6.73	£6.73
Contents insurance	£3.84	£3.84
Food	£35.00	£30.00
Clothes	£10.00	£10.00
Going out	£70.00	£10.00
Credit-card payments	£90.00	£40.00
Overdraft payments	£2.90	£0.00
Total spending	£279.34	£156.44
Shortfall/surplus	Shortfall of £96.14	Surplus of £26.76

3 Prioritise the debts Sean has just one priority debt – the rent. He has missed one monthly payment, so owes £215. His other debts are non-priority debts. Sean has £3,000 outstanding on his credit card. The minimum monthly repayments together come to around £90 and he's clocking up nearly £50 a month interest. Sean has also run up a £500 overdraft on his bank account.

4 Negotiate with creditors With the money advice centre's help, Sean writes to his landlord, credit-card issuer and bank, explaining that he has a problem repaying his debts and asking them to stop adding interest and charges while he clears the outstanding amounts.

The landlord agrees that Sean can clear the rent arrears at a rate of £50 a month (equivalent to £11.54 a week). This leaves just over £15 a week to set against the other debts. Sean apportions this between the overdraft and credit card according to the amount he owes, so $500/3,500 \times £15.22 = £2.17$ a week goes to the bank to clear the overdraft and 3,000/3,500 × £15.22 = £13.05 a week goes towards the credit card. It is not in the non-priority creditors' interest to turn down Sean's offer to make these repayments. If, instead, they took him to court, the court would simply freeze the interest and apportion the available money in much the same way. And, because they had turned down Sean's original reasonable offer, the court would not allow the creditors to recover their legal costs.

5 Open a new bank account The bank will automatically use any money coming into Sean's account to clear his overdraft. But the overdraft is not a priority debt and Sean needs to concentrate on paying the rent arrears if he is to avoid being evicted. So Sean opens a basic bank account at another bank and arranges for his earnings to be paid into the new account.

CHAPTER 7

Savings and investments

Whenever you have some spare cash or a lump sum that you don't need to use immediately, consider saving or investing it to make it grow. Collect £50 in a large glass bottle and you have £50. Put it in a savings account earning 4 per cent interest a year and, after five years, you'll have nearly £61.

This chapter outlines some of the savings and investment products you could choose. What will suit you best depends on a variety of factors, such as:

- your reason for saving
- how long you can leave your money and whether you might need it back in a hurry
- how you feel about risk
- your tax position.

Reasons for saving

If you still live at home, you might not have many demands on your income, so perhaps you can save from an allowance or Saturday earnings. You might be saving for something special – say, a shopping spree, buying Christmas presents, going on holiday with your mates, paying for driving lessons – or your savings might be more aimless. In most cases, you are probably looking at saving for the fairly short term, which is generally taken to mean fewer than five years. The most suitable products are likely to be bank and building society savings accounts and some of the National Savings & Investments (NS&I)* products.

Once you move away from home, you take greater financial responsibility for yourself. As a priority, consider building up an

Chart 7.1 Choosing savings and investments

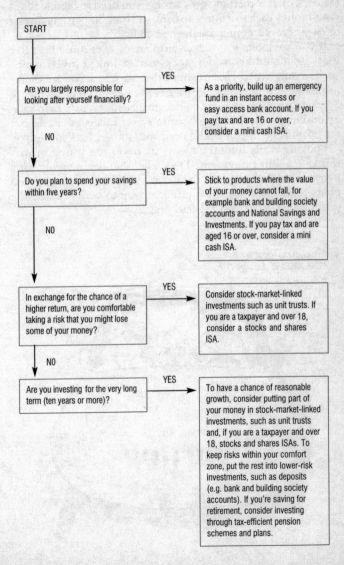

START

Are you largely responsible for looking after yourself financially? — **YES** → As a priority, build up an emergency fund in an instant access or easy access bank account. If you pay tax and are 16 or over, consider a mini cash ISA.

NO

Do you plan to spend your savings within five years? — **YES** → Stick to products where the value of your money cannot fall, for example bank and building society accounts and National Savings and Investments. If you pay tax and are aged 16 or over, consider a mini cash ISA.

NO

In exchange for the chance of a higher return, are you comfortable taking a risk that you might lose some of your money? — **YES** → Consider stock-market-linked investments such as unit trusts. If you are a taxpayer and over 18, consider a stocks and shares ISA.

NO

Are you investing for the very long term (ten years or more)? — **YES** → To have a chance of reasonable growth, consider putting part of your money in stock-market-linked investments, such as unit trusts and, if you are a taxpayer and over 18, stocks and shares ISAs. To keep risks within your comfort zone, put the rest into lower-risk investments, such as deposits (e.g. bank and building society accounts). If you're saving for retirement, consider investing through tax-efficient pension schemes and plans.

emergency fund – in other words, a cushion of money you can fall back on if something goes wrong. You need to be able to get your money back in a hurry, so bank and building society instant or easy-access accounts are the best choice.

If you are looking at longer-term saving over more than five years, you could consider stock-market-linked investments, such as unit trusts. This might be the case if, say, you are thinking about setting aside some money in case you go to university. Stock-market investments tend to give a better return than bank or building society savings accounts over longish periods, but are not suitable if you would need your money back in a hurry.

Looking really long term, you are never too young to start thinking about retirement. The earlier you begin saving for a pension, the less you need to save overall. Pension schemes and plans tend to be the most efficient way to save because the government offers you a special deal.

> **Example**
>
> Joe is 20 and, because he has a good income and few commitments at present, reckons it might be worth starting to save for his eventual retirement. Each £1,000 a year of pension (in today's money) he wants from age 65 will cost him just £10 a month if he starts saving now. If, on the other hand, he puts off starting to save until he reaches 30, he would need to save £16 a month for the same amount of pension.

How long you can leave your money

If you are saving for a large, long-term goal – say, you want to build up a lump sum to help you through university in eight years' time – you'd have to save a large sum each month if you relied on products such as bank and building society accounts, which tend to offer a fairly low rate of return – see Table 7.1.

Table 7.1 The amount you would need to save each month to build up a lump sum of £5,000 over eight years at different rates of return

If your yearly after-tax return averages this much:	12%	10%	8%	6%	4%	2%
You would need to save this much each month:	£32	£35	£38	£41	£44	£48

To reduce either the amount you need to save or the risk that your savings would fall short of your target, you could consider higher-risk investments, such as unit trusts, that tend to produce a higher rate of return over the long term. But, although the long-term trend may be upwards, the value of these investments can go down as well as up in the short term. You don't want to find that prices have slumped just at the time you need your money back. So, when you are within a few years of needing the money, you should consider locking in your returns by switching to safer investments, such as bank or building society accounts, the value of which cannot fall.

If you are saving only over a short period – fewer than five years – avoid stock-market investments altogether because there

may be too little time to ride out any slump in value, and so the
risk of losing your original money is too great.

How you feel about risk

Even if you are investing for the long term, think twice about
choosing stock-market-linked investments if you would be
worn to a frazzle worrying about losing your money. Stick to the
sort of investments and level of risk with which you feel
comfortable.

Your tax position

Everyone, even the youngest child, has tax allowances. For
example, in 2004–5, you can have £4,745 of income before you
have to pay any income tax. Similarly, you can have over £8,000
of gains from selling investments at a profit before you have to
pay any capital gains tax. This means that, if you have yet to start
working, you are probably a non-taxpayer. When it comes to
savings and investments, non-taxpayers should:

- arrange to receive interest from savings accounts 'gross' – in
  other words, without any tax deducted. Do this by filling in
  Form 85 available from the savings account provider
- consider those National Savings & Investments products
  that pay interest gross
- don't bother with tax-free investments, such as cash ISAs,
  unless the return offered is in any case higher than that from
  competing products
- try to avoid products, such as most investment-type life
  insurance, where tax has already been deducted and can't be
  reclaimed by you.

If you are a taxpayer, you should look at the return you will get
from your savings after any tax has been paid. It is also worth
considering tax-free products, such as ISAs, if you are eligible
for them.

  The next section describes the main savings and investments
you might consider, including how they are taxed.

How income tax works

Everyone can receive a certain amount of income each year completely tax-free. This is called your personal allowance. Any income above this amount is usually taxed. The first slice of taxable income is taxed at the starting rate (10 per cent in 2003–4). The next slice is taxed at the basic rate (10 per cent on dividends, 20 per cent on interest from savings and 22 per cent on other income) and anything more at the higher rate (32.5 per cent on dividends and 40 per cent on other income).

Some income is tax-free – for example, from cash ISAs – and ignored when working out your tax bill. Some other money you might receive does not count as income and so is not taxed – this includes student loans and other borrowing, and any money from your parents to cover your living expenses.

The return from many savings and investments is paid with some tax already deducted. If you are working, any other income tax you are due to pay is deducted direct from your pay (see Chapter 9). If these two routes do not collect all your tax, you'll usually have to fill in a tax return and pay the tax due through a system called self assessment.

Some savings and investments you might consider

Savings accounts

What are they? These are accounts offered by banks and building societies as a home for your money where it can grow by earning interest. With most accounts, the interest rate is variable (that is, it goes up and down in line with general interest rates). Some accounts provide a cash card so that you can draw your money out through cash machines.

How much must you save? With many accounts, no minimum and you choose when and how often to save.

When can you have your money back? Provided you choose an instant access or easy access account, you can have your money back at any time without giving notice.

How are they taxed? In general, interest from bank and building society accounts is paid with tax (at 20 per cent in 2003–4) already deducted. Non-taxpayers can claim back any tax already taken off – you would need to get form R40 from the Inland Revenue★ to do this. To save the hassle of claiming a refund, fill in form R85 from the bank or building society and you will be paid the interest in full with no tax deducted.

How do you shop around? Personal finance websites, magazines and sections in newspapers all regularly publish lists of the accounts offering the best rates of interest. The main organisation providing these comparison tables is Moneyfacts★.

How do you get started? Contact the bank or building society offering the account in which you are interested.

Cash ISAs

What are they? Savings accounts offered by banks, building societies and National Savings & Investments (NS&I). To be eligible, you must be aged 16 or over. Cash ISAs earn tax-free interest. With most accounts, the interest rate is variable.

How much must you save? With many accounts, no minimum and you choose when and how often to save.

When can you have your money back? Provided you choose an instant access or easy access ISA, you can have your money back at any time without giving notice.

How are they taxed? Tax-free.

How do you shop around? Personal finance websites, magazines and sections in newspapers all regularly publish lists of the accounts offering the best rates of interest. The main organisation providing these comparison tables is Moneyfacts★.

How do you get started? Contact the bank or building society concerned or NS&I.

How savings grow

When you put money in a savings account, it grows because interest is added.

The interest rate tells you, as a percentage, how much interest you'll get. A percentage is just a handy way of expressing fractions, as a given amount out of 100, so that they can be easily compared. For example, at 5 per cent interest, you would earn £5 interest over a whole year for every £100 in the account. If you had £50 in the account, that would be 5/100 × £50 = £2.50 interest over the year.

If you leave your interest to build up in the account, you benefit from 'compounding'. This means you earn interest on the interest as well as the amount originally paid in. For example, sticking with 5 per cent interest, if you start with £100 in your account, you'll have £105 at the end of year 1. The interest in year 2 will be 5/100 × £105 = £5.25, so you'll end the year with £110.25. In year 3, you'll earn 5/100 × £110.25 = £5.51, bringing your account balance up to £115.76, and so on. Over the three years, you haven't just earned interest of 3 × £5 = £15 – you've got an extra 76p because of compounding.

The example above assumes you are paid interest just once at the end of each year. But if the interest is added sooner – say, every six months – then you start to earn interest on the interest sooner and your money grows even more. Banks and building societies must tell you the interest rate in a standard way called an 'annual equivalent rate' or 'AER'. This takes into account when and how often interest is added to your account. You don't need to understand how the AER is worked out, just how to use it. If you are looking for an account that will pay you the most interest, compare the AERs. The account with the highest AER offers the best return.

NS&I Investment Account

What is it? This is a savings account offered by National Savings & Investments (NS&I). The interest rate is variable.

How much must you save? At least £10. You choose when and how often to add to the account.

When can you have your money back? At any time, but you must either give one month's notice or lose 30 days' interest.

How is it taxed? Interest is taxable but paid gross (without any tax deducted), which is very convenient if you are a non-taxpayer.

How do you shop around? Current rate available from NS&I* and Post Offices. Also often published in personal finance websites, magazines and sections in newspapers.

How do you get started? Contact NS&I or get a form from any Post Office.

NS&I Children's Bonus Bonds

What are they? These are savings bonds offered by National Savings & Investments (NS&I). You cannot buy them yourself, but, if you are under age 16, anyone over 16 can buy them for you. The bonds earn interest at a rate which is fixed for five years at a time. New interest rates are set on each fifth anniversary and you can continue holding the bonds until you reach age 21.

How much must you save? The bonds come in £25 units with a maximum investment of £1,000 per issue.

When can you have your money back? At any time, but no interest is paid if you cash in within the first year, and the interest is reduced unless you cash in on a fifth anniversary. Allow seven working days for payment to reach you.

How are they taxed? Tax-free.

How do you shop around? Current rate available from NS&I* and Post Offices. Also often published in personal finance websites, magazines and sections in newspapers.

How do you get started? The person making the investment for you should contact NS&I or get a form from any Post Office.

Premium Bonds

What are they? Premium Bonds are offered by National Savings & Investments (NS&I). But instead of earning interest, your bonds take part in a draw each month for prizes ranging from £50 up to £1 million. In December 2003, each £1 bond had a 1 in 30,000 chance of winning a prize each month.

How much must you save? At least £100.

When can you have your money back? At any time. Allow seven working days for payment to reach you.

How are they taxed? Prizes are tax-free.

How do you shop around? No need.

How do you get started? Contact NS&I or get a form from any Post Office.

Tax-efficient friendly society plans

What are they? These are stock-market-linked savings plans offered by friendly societies (which are similar to insurance companies). Unlike other stock-market-linked investments, these plans can be held by you direct even under the age of 18 (rather than held for you by an adult). Most often, someone else – for example, a parent or grandparent – takes out and pays into the plan for you. The money paid in gives you a stake in a fund of investments, the return on which depends wholly or partly on the performance of those investments.

How much must you save? This varies depending on the provider, but the maximum is only £25 a month or £270 a year. With such small amounts invested, charges often eat heavily into your return.

When can you have your money back? These plans are designed to run for at least 10 years and often longer, for example until you reach age 18. You can draw out money earlier, but the return is then usually very poor.

How are they taxed? Largely tax-free. You do not pay any tax on the payout. In addition, the friendly society does not pay tax on the return from the investments in the underlying fund, except that, from April 2004 onwards, the income from shares in the fund is due to be taxed at 10 per cent.

How do you shop around? Contact the providers direct for information or use an independent financial adviser (IFA)★. See occasional surveys in personal finance magazines, such as *Money Management*★. Consider also competing long-term investments, such as unit trusts, which although taxable have lower charges.

How do you get started? Contact providers direct or go to an IFA★.

Gifts from parents

There are special rules to prevent your parents from avoiding tax by shifting their money to you; however, these rules also catch many genuine gifts they might like to make. Under the rules, if a gift from a parent produces income of more than £100 a year, all the income is taxed as if it belongs to the parent rather than you. This applies all the time you are under age 18 and unmarried. However, the rules do not apply to gifts invested in NS&I Children's Bonus Bonds or tax-efficient friendly society plans. So, if mum or dad is worried about the tax angle, suggest they give you these as a way to build up a small nest egg.

Unit trusts

What are they? These are stock-market-linked investments. You can invest either regular sums or one-off lump sums. Your money gives you a stake in a fund of investments, typically shares. There are all sorts of different funds: for example, some invest just in the shares of UK companies; some invest in Japanese companies' shares; some invest for capital growth (being able to sell at a profit); some specialise in providing you with a regular income; and so on. The more specialist the fund, the more risky it tends to be. As a novice investor, it's often a good idea to start with a growth fund investing in UK companies, possibly a tracker fund – see *Tracker Funds*, opposite.

How much must you save? This varies depending on the provider, but usually £25 or £50 per month or £500 as a lump sum.

When can you have your money back? At any time. However, the value of your investment can fall as well as rise, so try to avoid cashing in at a time when the value has slumped.

How are they taxed? If the underlying fund invests in shares, any income paid out to you or reinvested is taxed at 10 per cent. Non-taxpayers can't reclaim this tax, but only higher-rate taxpayers have extra to pay. If the underlying fund is invested in corporate bonds and/or government bonds (gilts), any income paid out or reinvested is paid with 20 per cent tax already deducted. If you are a non-taxpayer, you can reclaim this. Higher-rate taxpayers have extra to pay. Any capital gains you make by selling your investment at a profit could in theory be taxed, but you can earn over £8,000 a year of such gains tax-free.

How do you shop around? Most personal finance websites, magazines and sections in newspapers list details about unit trusts. Some types are also covered in the Financial Services Authority (FSA) comparative tables★. A rich source of information is the Investment Management Association (IMA)★, especially its website, which includes an interactive questionnaire to narrow down your choice. Look for trusts that offer the type of return you want (growth, income or both), carry a risk level with which you feel comfortable, and preferably have low charges. When you have narrowed down your choice, obtain the Key Features Document (due to be replaced from mid-2004 by a similar Key Facts Document), which tells you the most important details about the trust in a set format that can easily be compared with other trusts. If you find it hard to decide on your own, consider getting help from an IFA.

How do you get started? The cheapest way to invest is often through a fund supermarket★ – a website where you can choose from many providers' wares and which often offers cut-price deals. Other options are to contact providers direct or go to an IFA.

Tracker funds

Investment funds, such as those available through unit trusts and pension schemes and plans, may be actively or passively managed. In an actively managed fund, the fund manager frequently trades the underlying investments, trying to pick the best-performing ones and the best times to buy and sell. In a passively managed fund – also called a tracker fund – the manager sets up the fund to mimic the performance of a particular stock-market index, such as the FTSE 100, and trades the underlying investments only as required to keep the fund on track. As a result, the dealing and management costs of a tracker fund tend to be much lower than for an actively managed fund and these cost savings can be passed on to you, the investor, in the form of lower charges.

Ethical investments

When you opt for an investment fund, by investing in, say, a unit trust or a personal pension, you have no control over the underlying investments in the fund – for example, the fund might be investing in the shares of companies involved in arms dealing or tobacco. If you prefer not to have your money supporting certain types of activity or want to be sure it is actively supporting good causes, ethical investment is for you. Different people have different ideas about what's ethical and what's not, but you can find lots of information to help you spot the investment funds that match your ethics by contacting the Ethical Investment Research Service (EIRIS)*.

Pension schemes and plans

What are they? These are products designed for saving up for retirement, with special tax treatment to encourage you to save. If you are working, your employer might run an occupational pension scheme and, assuming you are eligible to join it, this could be a good choice, because you'll get the benefit of money paid in on your behalf by your employer. If you don't have the option of an occupational scheme, consider saving through a stakeholder pension scheme or other personal pension – these are plans you arrange yourself with an insurance company. You choose how your contributions are invested. The choice is similar to the investment funds available through unit trusts (see pages 82–3).

How much must you save? Check at work how much you'd have to pay into any occupational scheme. Around 5 per cent of salary is common, with your employer typically paying in at least the same. With stakeholder schemes, the minimum can't be more than £20 either as a regular amount or lump sum and you can't be penalised for missing regular payments. The minimum may be higher for other types of personal pension.

When can you have your money back? Not until you reach a minimum age, which is currently 50 but expected to be set at 55 with effect from 2010.

How are they taxed? You get tax relief on what you pay into an occupational scheme; your savings build up largely tax-free and you can take part as a tax-free lump sum at retirement, though the rest must be taken as taxable pension. The tax breaks are similar for stakeholder schemes and other personal pensions, except, even if you are a non-taxpayer or pay tax at less than the basic rate, you still get basic-rate tax relief on contributions in the form of a bonus which is added to your scheme. This means that for every £10 you pay in, £12.82 is added to your scheme.

How do you shop around? For details of an occupational scheme, contact your human resources department at work. Many personal finance websites, magazines and sections in newspapers publish regular surveys of personal and stakeholder pensions. Stakeholder schemes are also covered in the FSA comparative tables*. When you have narrowed down your choice, obtain the Key Features Document (due to be replaced from mid-2004 by a similar Key Facts Document), which tells you the most important details about the scheme or plan in a set format that can easily be compared with other schemes. If you find it hard to make a choice on your own, consider getting help from an IFA*.

How do you get started? Contact providers direct or go to an IFA.

What are stakeholder pension schemes?

These are personal pensions which have been designed especially to offer value for money. To qualify for the name 'stakeholder', the scheme must include the following features:

- **low charges** No more than 1 per cent a year of the value of your fund, with no other charges
- **low and flexible contributions** Minimum set no higher than £20. Up to you when and how often you pay
- **portability** You can transfer to another pension scheme or plan without penalty
- **simplicity** There must be a default investment fund if you don't want to choose for yourself.

CHAPTER 8

Getting a job: your rights

You might decide to get a part-time job during your teenage years, or you might leave school at 16 to take up work, or you might manage to hold out until age 21 or later before entering the world of work. Whichever applies to you, the law gives you certain rights as an employee. Your main rights are outlined in this chapter. (Note that these rights do not apply if you work for yourself as a self-employed person or in partnership with others.)

When can you start work?

With very few exceptions, it is illegal for anyone to employ you before you reach age 13. Even then, you can't get just any job (see below). And, until you reach the statutory school-leaving age (see *Statutory school-leaving age*, below), your work must:

- be part-time
- be outside school hours, and
- not interfere with your school work.

Your local authority* is responsible for enforcing the laws about employing young people and making additional bye-laws that will apply if you work in that authority's area. If the laws or bye-laws are breached, your employer (but not you) can be fined. There is often a bye-law allowing children aged 10 and over to be employed on an occasional basis by their own parents in light agricultural or gardening work.

The rules apply whether you are paid or not, but only where you work for someone who aims to make profits. This means the rules do not apply to work that is not for profit, for example babysitting or helping a charity.

Illegal work

The rules are frequently overlooked by both employers and young people eager to earn a bit of money. The Low Pay Unit estimates that around two-thirds of children work illegally, usually because they are under age or working outside the permitted hours. However, bear in mind that the rules are there to protect you from unsuitable or dangerous work and exploitation. A good employer will comply with the rules and it is in your interests to work for a good employer.

Type of work if you are still at school

The law prohibits you from doing anything other than 'light work' or from working in dangerous industries if you are under the school-leaving age. Local authority bye-laws usually specify particular types of work that are prohibited. Typically, you are not allowed to:

- sell or deliver alcohol, cigarettes or tobacco
- work in a betting shop, amusement arcade, fairground or billiards or games club
- work in a cinema, theatre, disco, dance hall or night club
- work in a petrol station
- work in a commercial kitchen or undertake food preparation
- deliver milk
- call at houses to collect money
- collect or sort refuse
- work in telesales
- work in a dangerous occupation or near dangerous machinery
- work in a slaughterhouse or butcher's shop
- provide personal care in a residential or nursing home
- lift, move or carry heavy objects
- clean windows externally above the ground floor or do any other job that involves working at heights greater than 3 metres.

There are additional restrictions on the type of work you can do if you are under age 14, when you are only allowed to take on the following jobs:

- office work
- delivering newspapers
- working in a shop or hairdresser's
- working at a riding stables
- light work in a café or restaurant (for example, waiting at tables, but not kitchen work)
- light agricultural or gardening work
- car washing by hand in a residential area
- domestic work in a hotel or guest house.

Under age 14, you may also work in areas such as sport, advertising, theatre and film, provided your employer has a licence from the local authority.

Statutory school-leaving age

The statutory school-leaving age is the earliest date at which you can legally leave school. It is the last Friday in June of the school year in which you reach age 16.

Hours of work

While under school-leaving age, there are restrictions on the hours you can work. You may *not* work:

- on school days, during school hours (including your lunch break)
- before 7am or after 7pm
- on school days and Sundays, for more than two hours; on school days, this may include a maximum of one hour before school
- on Saturdays and holidays, for more than five hours if you are under 15, or eight hours otherwise
- during school holidays, more than 25 hours a week if you are under 15, or 35 hours otherwise.

Once you are over school-leaving age, you can work full-time. In theory, your working week cannot be more than 48 hours unless you have agreed to work the longer hours. In practice, it might be hard to refuse longer hours if there is a long-hours culture in your workplace or refusal might affect, say, your promotion prospects. Regardless of how many hours you work each week, a working day should normally be no longer than 13 hours.

Breaks and holidays

If you work for more than four hours a day, you should be given a one-hour break if you are under school-leaving age or 30 minutes if you are older but under age 18. If you are 18 or over, you usually have the right to a 20-minute break after six hours of work.

From school-leaving age until you reach 18, you are entitled to 48 hours off every seven days. Once you reach 18, you have the right to one uninterrupted rest day in every seven days, or two rest days in a span of 14 days.

During the school holidays, you should be given a two-week break from work, if you are under school-leaving age, but you have no right to paid holiday.

Over school-leaving age, you have the right to four weeks' paid holiday a year if you work full time and a pro-rata amount if you work part-time. For example, if you work just one day a week, you are entitled to four days' paid holiday during the year.

Sick pay

Below school-leaving age, you are not entitled to sick pay if you're off work because of illness. Above school-leaving age, you have the right to receive statutory sick pay from your employer if you are unable to work because of illness, provided various conditions are met. The conditions include: you earn above a set amount (£79 a week in 2004–5), and are off sick for more than three consecutive days. Your employer might have more generous sick-pay arrangements and, if so, these will be set out in your written statement (see page 91).

Work permit

If you do paid or unpaid work while you are under school-leaving age, local authority bye-laws normally require you to have a work permit from your local authority. You get a permit by filling in a form available from your employer, your school or the local authority. Your employer fills in the first part of the form and a parent or guardian fills in the second part. You then return the form to your local authority.

If the local authority is satisfied that the job conforms with the rules for young people and that proper health and safety procedures are being followed, a permit will be sent to your employer. The permit remains valid until:

- you leave that job (if you are taking up a new job and you are still under school-leaving age, you'll need to apply for a new permit)
- you reach the statutory school-leaving age
- it is withdrawn, perhaps because your parents are concerned about the impact of the job on you or your school work.

If your job changes – for example, you start working longer hours – you are required to tell your local authority.

You do not need a work permit to do work that is not for profit, such as babysitting or helping a charity. And you do not need a work permit to do work experience arranged by your school.

National minimum wage

There is no national minimum wage for people under 18 and often the pay on offer will be pretty low. You'll have to decide whether you are prepared to work for low pay, for example to build up some work experience or because there are no better-paid jobs available locally.

Once you reach 18, you are covered by the national minimum wage law and, in the year from October 2003, the lowest amount you can be paid is:

- £3.80 per hour if you are under 22
- £4.50 per hour if you are aged 22 or over.

If you are not getting at least the minimum wage, feel you should be and want to get the problem sorted out, you can contact the National Minimum Wage Helpline*.

The national minimum wage does not apply to everyone. For example, it will not apply if you are self-employed, a volunteer, or a student working as part of your course. It does not generally apply in apprenticeships.

Contracts and written statements

You'll sometimes hear people say, 'I haven't been given a contract'. In fact, a contract of employment exists the minute you start work, though it may be just an oral (spoken) contract. Usually, the fact of your starting work is taken as proof that you have accepted the terms and conditions offered by the employer.

However, within two months of starting work, you should have been given a written statement that sets out the main terms and conditions of your contract. (You don't have this right if your employment is to be for less than a month.)

Among other details, the written statement should include the name of your employer, the date you started work, your job title or a brief job description, your pay, hours of work and holiday entitlement, arrangements for sick leave and any sick pay, your place of work and, if the job is not permanent, the expected duration of the job or date it will end.

If you have a problem at work, such as being expected to do large amounts of unpaid overtime, or being paid late or too little, you'll find it much easier to take up such issues with your employer if you have your terms and conditions in writing. So, if you have not been given a written statement automatically, make a point of asking for one. If your employer refuses to give you a statement, you can refer the problem to an employment tribunal★.

Itemised pay statement

You are also entitled to a pay statement, which must be given to you at the time you are paid or before. Chapter 9 looks at what your pay statement must show and what it all means. If your employer fails to give you pay statements, and does not start doing so when you ask for them, you can take your complaint to an employment tribunal.

Babysitting

There is no statutory minimum age requirement relating to babysitting, but being responsible for children is a big job, which should not be taken on lightly. The Royal Society for the Prevention of Accidents recommends that babysitters should be aged at least 16. The Red Cross, which runs training courses for babysitters, requires participants to have reached age 14 by the time they take their final assessment.

If you decide to become a babysitter, get some training, for example from the British Red Cross* or St John Ambulance*. You should familiarise yourself with the home you are visiting and try to identify potential hazards. If possible, have some back-up available, such as a parent on whom you can call if you run into problems, and always make sure you have a contact number for the parents or guardians of the child you are looking after. You should also ensure that you have arrangements for getting back home safely.

CHAPTER 9

Understanding your pay slip

If you work, your employer is by law required to give you a pay slip at (or before) the time you are paid. These days, the pay will usually be transferred direct to your bank account and you'll be given the pay slip separately at work.

The pay slip helps you to keep a check on what you have been paid, whether the amount is correct, and why various deductions have been made. You should always check the slip and immediately raise any queries with your boss or the accounts department at work if there is one.

The law sets out what must be included on your pay slip but does not specify any particular format, so the appearance of pay slips will vary from one employer to another. Chart 9.1 shows a typical slip. The various entries are then explained, and how they are worked out. It is based on the example of Jenny Chiplan, 19, who works full-time in a cybercafé, helping to prepare food, serving and taking money. She earns £3.80 an hour and normally works 38 hours a week. She is paid monthly.

Tax year

Everything to do with tax is worked out in relation to tax years. A tax year runs from 6 April to the following 5 April.

Chart 9.1 Example of a pay slip

EMPLOYEE NAME					EMPLOYEE NUMBER
JENNY CHIPLAN					03 (A)
BASIC	OVERTIME	BONUS/OTHER PAY	PAY PERIOD		DATE
£625.67 (B)	£0.00		10 (C)		31/1/04
EMPLOYEE NIC	DEDUCTION 1	DEDUCTION 2	TAX CODE		TAX THIS PERIOD
£26.48 (D)			461L (E)		£33.37 (F)
EMPLOYER NIC	GROSS PAY	PENSION DEDUCTION	TOTAL DEDUCTIONS		NET PAY
£30.82 (G)	£625.67 (H)	£20.00 (I)	£79.85 (J)		£545.82 (K)

DUMTOWN CYBERCAFÉ

What each item means

(A) Employee number

Especially if you work for a large employer, you will be given an employee or works number that is specific to you. This is used to locate your records correctly, so you should quote it whenever you need to contact your employer about your pay.

(B) Basic

This shows the basic amount you are being paid for the period covered by the slip (one month in this case). If you have earned extra through overtime, bonuses, and so on, this may be shown separately. The total of basic pay and extras is the amount of gross pay (see H below). In this example, Jenny just has basic pay of £625.67 and no extras.

(C) Pay period

When you work for an employer, the tax year is divided into pay periods. The number of periods depends on how often you are paid. If you are paid weekly, there will be 52 pay periods. If you are paid monthly, there will be 12. Each period is numbered, starting with the one that covers 6 April. In this example, Jenny is being paid for the tenth month in the tax year (January 2004).

(D) Employee NIC

You do not receive the full amount of gross pay (H) because various deductions are taken off. Unless your earnings are too low, one of the deductions will be for National Insurance contributions. Both you and your employer pay these contributions – see *National Insurance*, on page 101. This entry shows the amount you must pay. Your employer must deduct this amount from your earnings before they are paid over to you. It is important to check that your contributions have been paid because they affect your entitlement to claim various state benefits, such as Jobseeker's Allowance if you become unemployed and state pension when many years ahead you reach retirement.

(E) Tax code

If you earn enough to be liable for income tax (see *Income tax* overleaf), your employer must also deduct the tax from your earnings before they are paid to you. The tax code is used by your employer to work out the correct amount to deduct. See *PAYE and tax codes*, on page 102, for how your tax code is used.

(F) Tax this period

This shows the amount of income tax that your employer has deducted from your pay.

(G) Employer NIC

Unless your earnings are too low, your employer must pay National Insurance contributions on what he or she pays you (see *National Insurance*, on page 101). This is a separate cost that your employer bears direct and is not deducted from your pay. In this example, the cost to Jenny's employer of employing her is her gross pay plus the employer NIC, that is, £625.67 + £30.82 = £656.49.

(H) Gross pay

This is the amount of pay you would get if there were no deductions.

(I) Pension deduction

You might be paying into a pension scheme as a way of saving for retirement. This could be an occupational scheme run by your employer. Alternatively, it might be a personal pension or stakeholder scheme if there is an arrangement through work for contributions to be deducted direct from your pay. If you are young, or if this is just a Saturday or holiday job, you probably will not be making any pension contributions, so there will be £0 in this box. But, once you have a permanent job, it is usually a good idea to start contributions if you can. See Chapter 7 for more information about pension savings. In this example, Jenny is paying £20 a month into a stakeholder scheme. Her employer deducts the contributions straight from her pay and hands them over to the pension provider.

(J) Total deductions

This is the sum of all the deductions – for example, for your own (but not your employer's) National Insurance contributions, income tax and pension. The total should be the difference between your gross pay (H) and your net pay (K).

(K) Net pay

This is your pay after all deductions have been subtracted and is the amount that should actually go into your bank account or, if you are paid in cash, handed over to you. Sometimes, your pay is split with, say, part being paid in cash and part direct to your bank. In this case, your pay slip should state how much is being paid by each method.

Income tax

You might have to pay income tax whatever your age, but only if you have a taxable income above a certain amount. Some types of income are tax-free, such as interest from Children's Bonus Bonds, and student grants, loans and scholarships. Most types of income, including earnings from a job, are taxable. But there's no tax to pay if your yearly income does not exceed your personal allowance (£4,745 in 2004–5).

If your taxable income is bigger than your personal allowance, you will have tax to pay as shown in Table 9.1. If you have a job, your employer collects the tax for you and hands it over to the Inland Revenue (the government department responsible for most taxes) – see *PAYE and tax codes,* on page 102.

THE 'L' IN MY TAX CODE STANDS FOR "LOW PAID!"

Table 9.1 Income tax allowances and rates in 2003–4

	Yearly amount	Monthly equivalent	Weekly equivalent	Main rate of tax on this part of your income
Personal allowance (the amount of taxable income you can have before you start to pay tax)	£4,615 [1]	£385	£89	0%
Starting-rate band (the next slice of your income after the personal allowance)	£1,960	£163	£38	10%
Basic-rate band (the next slice of your income after the starting-rate band)	£28,540	£2,378	£549	22%
Higher-rate band (all the rest of your income after the bands above)	No limit	No limit	No limit	40%

[1] The personal allowance increases to £4,745 in 2004–5. Tax bands and rates for 2004–5 had not been published at the time of writing.

> **Example**
>
> Steve works in a garage and earns £9,000 a year. He has no other income. In 2003–4, his tax bill is worked out as follows:
>
> - first £4,615 (his personal allowance) is tax-free
> - next £1,960 is taxed at 10 per cent, i.e. 10% × £1,960 = £196.00
> - the remaining £2,425 is taxed at 22 per cent, i.e. 22% × £2,425 = £533.50.
>
> In total, Steve pays £196.00 + £533.50 = £729.50 income tax on his pay of £9,000.

Non-taxpayer

If you just have a Saturday or evening job it is unlikely that you will earn enough to have to pay tax. Your weekly or monthly pay will be below the amount of personal allowance and so your employer will hand over your pay without any deduction for income tax.

If you are a student and work during your holidays, you might earn more than the monthly or weekly equivalent of the personal allowance during the period you work, in which case your employer would normally deduct some income tax. But, if your income for the year as a whole is less than your personal allowance, you should not be paying tax at all. In this situation, you could claim back any tax deducted, but there is another option. Provided you are sure that your income for the whole year will be less than your personal allowance, you can arrange for your employer to pay you without deducting any income tax. To do this, get form P38(S) from your employer or your local Tax Office★. Fill in the back and return it to your employer.

If you have paid too much tax

If you are a non-taxpayer, you can usually arrange to receive income from work (see above) and savings (see Chapter 7) without any tax deducted. Nevertheless, sometimes you will receive income that has already been taxed and may need to claim the tax back.

Similarly, even though you should correctly pay some tax (for example, because you are a starting-rate taxpayer), you may have received income with too much tax deducted, in which case you will be eligible to claim a refund.

If you have paid too much income tax and you are working, tell your employer. To claim back tax overpaid on earnings after you have stopped work, get form P50 from your local Tax Office. To claim back tax overpaid on savings or investments, ask for form R40.

National Insurance

National Insurance contributions (NICs) are another form of tax, but have a special significance because the record of payments you build up can entitle you to claim certain state benefits. These include Jobseeker's Allowance (if you become unemployed), incapacity benefit (if you fall ill) and state pension (when you eventually retire). In some circumstances, you are treated as if you have paid contributions even though you have paid nothing.

NICs are due only on earned income, not on income from, for example, savings or investments. If you are an employee, your employer deducts your NICs direct from your pay and hands them over to the Inland Revenue.

You pay NICs only during your 'working life', which is age 16 up to state pension age (65 for everyone retiring after 2020). So, if you are under 16 and working, your employer should not deduct any NICs from your pay. Your employer is legally required to start accounting for NICs once you reach age 16, although there is no legal requirement for you to tell your employer that you have had your sixteenth birthday. Therefore, when you first start your job, you may find that your employer asks for your date of birth or even to see your birth certificate.

> **No NICs**
>
> You do not pay National Insurance contributions if you are under age 16 or if you are doing a job that is exempt, which applies to a newspaper round if you are still at school and work experience arranged by your school.

Once you reach 16, you may have to pay NICs but only if you earn at least a certain amount, called the 'primary threshold' (£91 a week in 2004–5). Above that threshold, you normally pay contributions as shown in Table 9.2. Your employer also has to pay NICs on your earnings, but these contributions are just a straightforward tax and do not affect your eligibility for state benefits.

There are different types of NICs. The type paid by employees and employers is called Class 1 National Insurance.

Table 9.2 National Insurance contributions paid by employees [1] in 2004–5

Band of earnings	Weekly amount	Monthly equivalent	Yearly equivalent	Main rate of NICs you pay on this band of earnings	Do NICs on this band help you claim state benefits?
Up to the lower earnings limit (£79 a week)	£79	£343	£4,108	No NICs payable	No
Above lower earnings limit and up to primary threshold (£91 a week)	£12	£53	£637	0%	Yes
Above primary threshold and up to the upper earnings limit (£610 a week)	£519	£2,248	£26,975	11%	Yes
Rest of your earnings above the upper earnings limit	No limit	No limit	No limit	1%	No

[1] Aged 16 or over. You do not pay NICs under age 16, however much you earn.

PAYE and tax codes

Your employer is required by law to act as a tax collector for the government by deducting the income tax and NICs due on

---

Example

In 2004–5 Steve, who works in a garage and earns £9,000 a year, pays Class 1 NICs on his earnings as follows:

- first £4,108 (lower earnings limit) – no NICs
- next £637 (up to the primary threshold) is taxed at 0 per cent, so again no NICs
- remaining £4,255 is taxed at 11 per cent, i.e. 11% × £4,255 = £468.05.

---

your pay and handing the correct amounts over to the Inland Revenue on a regular basis. The Revenue helps your employer to do this by providing a tax code for each employee. This system is known as Pay-as-you-earn, or PAYE.

Usually around January each year, you will receive a Notice of Coding which tells you the tax code that will be provided to your employer for use in the tax year starting in April and how the code has been worked out.

The notice of coding sets out your tax-free allowance and any adjustments needed to:

- collect tax underpaid or refund tax overpaid in the past
- collect extra tax on, say, untaxed savings, taxable fringe benefits, or a second job, and
- give relief for, say, expenses that qualify for tax relief.

These are added together and the last digit knocked off. When the code is used by your employer, the last digit is added back to find the amount of tax-free pay you should have. In fact, it is always a '9' that is added to ensure that you are not short-changed. This means you often get a few pounds of extra tax allowance. For example, if your code is 474L, the first £4,749 of your income will be tax-free. If you are paid monthly, you get 1/12 of this amount tax-free each pay period. If you are paid weekly, you get 1/52. The letter in your tax code – in this case 'L' – tells your employer about your tax allowance or tax rate. See Table 9.3 for examples of codes you are most likely to come across.

Having deducted your tax-free pay, the correct amounts of income tax and NICs are calculated by your employer using tax tables supplied by the Inland Revenue (either in paper form or built into a computer program).

Table 9.3 Example of letters used in tax codes

Letter	What it means
L	You get the personal allowance for a person under 65
BR	All your income is taxed at the basic rate (usually used where you have a second job and your tax allowances have already been set against earnings from the other job)
0T	None of this income is tax-free, but tax starts to be deducted at the starting rate (usually used where you have a second job and your tax allowances have already been set against earnings from the other job)
NT	No tax is deducted from this income, usually because your total income is less than your tax-free allowance
T	Your affairs are more complicated or you have asked your Tax Office not to use any of the other codes

---

Example

In January 2004, Jenny Chiplan earns £625.67 before tax (see the pay slip on page 95). Her tax code (amount E on the pay slip) is 461L. This tells her employer that she should have £4,619 a year of pay tax-free. Jenny is paid monthly, so she gets £4,619/12 = £384.92 a month of pay tax-free. Tax that month on the remaining £625.67 − £384.92 = £240.75 comes to £33.37 (amount F on the pay slip).

New job

In most jobs, you are paid monthly or weekly. If you work for a full tax year, getting $1/12$ or $1/52$ of the annual tax-free pay each pay period is fine and should result in the correct amount of tax being paid. But if you work for only part of the tax year, you will get less than the full amount of tax-free pay and so end up paying too much tax. To avoid this problem, when you first start work or change jobs, you give your new employer the information needed to adjust the amount in your pay packet to ensure that the correct tax has been paid.

The information is given on form P46 if you are starting your first job since leaving full-time education or the first job you've had after a longish break. Your employer should provide the form.

When you leave a job, your old employer should provide you with a form P45. This summarises the tax and NICs you have paid so far during the tax year. You give your copy of form P45 to your new employer when you start your new job (or to the Jobcentre Plus★ office if you are claiming benefits).

Working for yourself

You might decide to start your own business. If so, the easiest way to organise your work is likely to be as a self-employed person. Any profits you make count as taxable income and you'll be liable for income tax if your total taxable income from all sources comes to more than your personal allowance. You'll have no employer to collect the tax through PAYE, so you have to arrange to pay the tax yourself via a system called self assessment.

Most self-employed people have to register their business with the Inland Revenue within three months of the end of the month in which they start up, or risk a fine of £100. But, if you are not liable to pay NICs because you are under age 16, this requirement does not apply.

Once you reach 16, you come within the NICs system. You do not have to pay NICs if your profits are less than a set amount (£4,215 a year in 2004–5). However, this exemption is not given automatically – you have to apply to the Inland Revenue. Contact the Tax Office that deals with you normally or, if you don't yet have one, contact any local Tax Office.

For more information, contact the Inland Revenue's Helpline for the Newly Self-employed★, visit the Revenue website or see Inland Revenue booklet P/SE/1 *Starting your own business.*

CHAPTER 10

Your finances as a student

According to the research group Roar, almost half of people at or considering university are worried about the amount they will owe by the time they graduate. Nonetheless, current surveys find that, despite debts, graduates do not regret going to university. But with an increase in tuition fees on the cards, will this still be the case in future? Just what are the costs and debts you might face and what financial help can you expect?

The rewards

A government report says that graduates on average earn around 50 per cent more than people without degrees, are only half as likely to be unemployed, and have had twice as many job promotions over the last five years.

What does it cost to be a student?

The big picture

A government-commissioned survey of students' income and expenditure during the 2002–3 academic year found that, on average, students were spending just under £6,900 a year. This can be roughly carved into three chunks:

- **housing** (£1,281 a year) which includes rent, retainers to keep a room until term starts and you move in, and other housing-related costs
- **participation** (£960), meaning the costs of taking part in the course including tuition fees, books, travel to lectures, and so on
- **living** (£4,656), covering food, household goods, personal spending, entertainment and travel other than to and from university.

Chart 10.1 shows in more detail how the costs were made up. The biggest individual items of spending were entertainment (with a lion's share being spent on alcohol), rent, personal expenses (of which a significant chunk went on mobile phone calls) and food.

There was a big variation in overall spending for students studying in London (where you can expect to spend nearly £7,835 a year) compared with those studying outside London (£6,691 a year).

Chart 10.1 How students spend their money

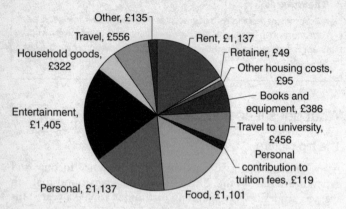

Source: *2002/03 Student Income and Expenditure Survey*, survey commissioned by
Department for Education and Skills, Research report 487.

Therefore, assuming costs rise on average by, say, 2.5 per cent
each year, if you intended to start a university course in autumn
2004, you could expect to spend in excess of £22,000 over a
period of three years – and more if increased tuition fees were
added in.

Accommodation

One obvious way to save money would be to continue living at
home and to attend a local university if there is one available.
But, surprisingly, the survey did not show a very large decline in
overall spending as a result of living with parents:

- students living with parents spent £6,731 in total
- students in university-provided accommodation spent
  £6,658, and
- students in other rented accommodation spent £7,117.

The undoubted saving on accommodation costs was eroded by higher costs of travelling to and from university, with students living at home spending on average £814 a year on travel costs compared with £261 for students in university-provided accommodation and £408 for students in other rented accommodation. Students living at home also spent more than other students on books and computer equipment, perhaps so that they could study efficiently from home.

Tuition fees – England and Wales

Under the system in place at the time of writing, students and/or their parents must normally pay £1,125 a year towards the cost of tuition fees. (The remaining cost is picked up by taxpayers.) These fees must be paid upfront at the start of each academic year, so you or your family may have to pay out around £3,375 in total during a three-year period of study.

However, the £1,125 contribution is means-tested, so poorer families pay less or nothing at all. How much must be paid depends on:

- your own income if you have any, but ignoring various amounts including any earnings from casual or part-time jobs you do while studying and during the holidays, and the first £4,000 from any scholarship, sponsorship or similar award
- your parents' 'residual income', which is their before-tax income less various allowances, including what they pay into pension schemes.

If your parents' residual income is less than £20,970 in 2003–4, there is nothing to pay towards tuition fees. If their income is £31,230 or more, they will be expected to pay the full £1,125. Between these two limits, only part of the fee is payable – see Table 10.1 below for examples.

The parental contribution is reduced by £83 for each brother or sister you have who is still dependent on your parents.

Although your parents are expected to pay the relevant amount of tuition fee, there is no mechanism to force them to

Table 10.1 How much parents are expected to pay towards tuition fees in the 2003–4 academic year

Residual income		Contribution to tuition fees
Less than	£20,970	£0
	£20,970	£45
	£21,000	£48
	£22,000	£153
	£23,000	£259
	£24,000	£364
	£25,000	£469
	£26,000	£574
	£27,000	£680
	£28,000	£785
	£29,000	£890
	£30,000	£996
	£31,000	£1,101
	£31,230 or more	£1,125

do so. If your parents can't or won't pay, you have to find the payment yourself.

At the time of writing, the equivalent figures for the 2004–5 and 2005–6 academic years had not been published, but were expected to be similar to those described here for 2003–4 with just a smallish increase in line with inflation.

For students starting university from 2006–7 onwards, the system is due to change. At the time of writing, Parliament had narrowly accepted the government's proposals in principle. The proposed new system is described below, although the details could be changed as the legislation makes its way through Parliament. You can check the position by visiting the website of the Department for Education and Skills (DfES)*.

The intention is that the amount you pay towards tuition fees (called 'top-up fees') will be:

- **variable and in many cases higher** Universities will be able to charge any amount from £0 to £3,000 a year. Elite universities are expected to opt for higher fees. Within the same university, fees may vary from one course to another with, for example, low fees being charged for courses that are undersubscribed where the university wants to attract more students

- **capped until 2010** Apart from increases in line with inflation, the government has said it will not raise the £3,000 a year upper limit on fees during the next term of Parliament (if the Labour Party is re-elected). This has disappointed universities that would like to charge more
- **deferred** Instead of paying fees at the start of each year during your course, you will borrow the amount through a new Graduate Contribution Scheme and repay it only after graduation and once earnings exceed a set threshold (probably £15,000 a year). You will then repay at a rate of 9 per cent of your income above the threshold (but can make larger repayments if you want to). The repayments will be collected through the tax system
- **subsidised** In the case of students from low-income backgrounds with the first £1,125 (or possibly more) being paid by the government
- **reviewed in 2009** The review will also examine whether higher fees are affecting recruitment to the professions (such as law) and whether maintenance grants could be extended to more students.

Tuition fees – Scotland

There is no parental contribution towards tuition fees if both your home and place of study are in Scotland. Instead, you may have to pay a Graduate Endowment after graduation. This is a one-off, lump-sum payment, currently around £2,000. You can take out a student loan (see below) to cover this payment.

What financial help is available for students?

The government-sponsored survey of students' spending also looked at their sources of income in 2002–3. Chart 10.2 summarises the position for the average student.

On average, students had an income of £5,513, of which just under half (£2,677) came from student loans and other student support schemes.

Chart 10.2 Where students get their money

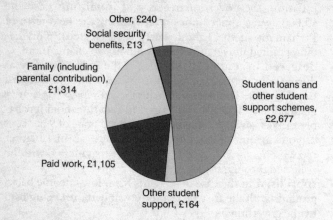

Other, £240
Social security benefits, £13
Family (including parental contribution), £1,314
Student loans and other student support schemes, £2,677
Paid work, £1,105
Other student support, £164

Source: *2002/03 Student Income and Expenditure Survey*, survey commissioned by Department for Education and Skills, Research report 487.

Student loans

Student loans are designed to help you with your living costs while a student. Table 10.2 shows the maximum loans available in 2003–4. At the time of writing, amounts for 2004–5 and subsequent years had yet to be published. The government had announced that it was reviewing the amounts with a view to increasing them if they were found insufficient to cover student costs of living.

A quarter of the maximum loan is available only to students from a low-income background, and the available amount from this is based on your own income (if any) and your parents' residual income as defined already on page 109. If their residual income is £31,230 or less, they are expected to pay towards your tuition fees, but nothing towards your living costs. Table 10.3 below shows the amount they are expected to pay towards both tuition fees and living costs combined, depending on their residual income. However, there is no way to make your parents pay the contribution. If they can't or won't pay, you'll have to either find the money yourself or tighten your belt a bit more.

Table 10.2 Maximum student loans available in 2003–4

	Overall maximum available	Maximum non-means-tested amount	Maximum means-tested amount
Full-year rates (i.e. each year apart from the final year)			
Living away from home and studying in London	£4,930	£3,695	£1,235
Living away from home and studying elsewhere	£4,000	£3,000	£1,000
Living at your parents' home	£3,165	£2,375	£790
Final-year rates			
Living away from home and studying in London	£4,275	£3,205	£1,070
Living away from home and studying elsewhere	£3,470	£2,605	£865
Living at your parents' home	£2,765	£2,070	£695

The remaining three-quarters of the maximum student loan is available regardless of your income.

You do not have to borrow the maximum amount, but in general it will be worth doing so (see *How to apply for a student loan*, overleaf). You will normally receive each year's loan in three tranches, one at the start of each term.

You do not start to repay your student loans until after the end of your course and the loans are 'income contingent'. This means you make repayments only if your income exceeds a set threshold, currently £10,000 a year but likely to rise to £15,000 from 2005. You repay at a rate of 9 per cent of your income above the threshold. Repayments are collected through the tax system. You can make larger repayments if you want to.

There is no interest as such on the money you owe in student loans. Instead, the amount outstanding is increased each year in line with inflation. This means student loans will generally be a good deal cheaper than any other form of borrowing.

For loans taken out under the current system, any amount still outstanding when you reach age 65 is written off. Under

How to apply for a student loan

For information about student loans and other financial help for students, contact the Student Loans Company* or visit the website of Student Finance Direct*. To apply, if you live in:

- **England and Wales**, contact your Local Education Authority*. In future, you will also be able to apply online through the Student Finance Direct website
- **Scotland**, contact the Student Awards Agency for Scotland*. You can apply online at www.student-support-saas.gov.uk
- **Northern Ireland**, contact your Local Education and Library Board*.

Table 10.3 How much parents are expected to pay towards your combined tuition and living costs in 2003–4 [1]

Residual income	Contribution to tuition fees and living costs
£31,230 [2]	£1,125
£32,000	£1,206
£33,000	£1,311
£34,000	£1,417
£35,000	£1,522
£36,000	£1,627
£37,000	£1,732
£38,000	£1,838
£38,735	£1,915 [3]
£39,000	£1,943
£40,000	£2,048
£40,730	£2,125 [4]
£41,000	£2,153
£42,000	£2,259
£42,963 or more	£2,360 [5]

[1] In a full year – slightly lower amounts apply in your final year.
[2] Where residual income is £20,970 or more, they will be expected to pay towards tuition costs as shown on page 110.
[3] Maximum contribution if you live at home with your parents.
[4] Maximum contribution if you live away from home outside London.
[5] Maximum contribution if you live away from home and in London.

the new system from 2006, any amount still not repaid will be written off after 25 years.

Other student support schemes

You may be eligible for extra money from the Student Loans Company* or your Local Education Authority if you have children or support a dependent adult, you have a disability, or you were living in care prior to starting your course.

If your income is low, you may be able to get an Access to Learning Grant from your college. Contact your college's student services department for details.

The government has also announced that from August 2004 onwards it intends to reintroduce student grants for people from low-income families. Under the new scheme, students whose families earn less than £10,000 a year will be eligible for a grant of probably £1,500 a year.

To encourage a supply of graduates to fill key public-sector jobs, the government funds various financial packages for people training to be:

- **teachers** No tuition fee for postgraduate certificate of education (PGCE) courses. Teachers' student loans are written off over ten years if teaching a shortage subject
- **doctors and dentists** Government meets fees for fifth and later years of courses
- **nurses, midwives and allied health professionals** No tuition fees
- **social work** Fees met by government.

As part of the package of changes to tuition fees planned from 2006, the government will require universities to use part of their increased fee income to make more bursaries available to low-income students.

Paid work

According to the government-sponsored survey of student incomes and spending, seven out of ten students work to supplement their income while studying. Nearly six out of ten worked during term time, working on average ten hours a week (though the hours were often erratic from one week to the next). One in five students worked more than 20 hours a week.

Around 85 per cent of students worked during the summer vacation.

Why it might be better if your family did not support you too much

Parents often worry more than you about you eventually entering the workforce with massive debts. If they can afford it, they may be tempted to finance a substantial chunk of your costs as a student. Fortunate though you would be, this strategy does not necessarily make financial sense.

As they stand, student loans are one of the cheapest forms of loan available. The interest on a student loan (which is set at the rate of inflation) is currently lower than the interest your parents can earn on their savings or would pay on borrowing. So it would not make sense for them to cash in their savings or borrow to fund you through university. It would be better if you took up the maximum student loans for now. Your parents can leave their money invested with a view to clearing your loans later on.

Even later on, it would not make sense to pay off your student loans if instead you or your parents would be taking out more expensive forms of borrowing, such as an overdraft, credit-card debt or a mortgage. Instead, your parents might be willing to clear your overdraft or card debts or give you a deposit towards buying a home to reduce the amount you need to borrow as a mortgage.

Similarly, it could be more cost-effective after graduation for your parents to invest money for you rather than pay off your student loans. For example, they could pay into a pension plan for you, or pay contributions to top up your state pension – see *Top up your state pension*, below.

Bear in mind, too, that after graduation you might get a job with an employer who is willing to pay off your student debts as an incentive for you to take the job.

On a more sombre note, student loans are written off if you die, become permanently disabled or reach state pension age. Under the new system from 2006, they will also be written off after 25 years.

Top up your state pension

The amount of state basic pension you will eventually receive will depend on the record of National Insurance contributions you have built up over your whole working life from age 16 to 65. The years when you are at university appear as gaps in your record and may reduce the pension you get. You can fill these gaps by paying voluntary Class 3 National Insurance contributions. You have up to six years after the end of each contribution year (which runs from 6 April to the following 5 April) to make these payments, after which the opportunity is lost. For more information, see Inland Revenue leaflet CA08 *Voluntary National Insurance contributions* available from the Inland Revenue website (*www.inlandrevenue.gov.uk/nic/index.htm*) or your local Tax Office*.

Student debts

You don't need a degree in maths to work out that, if students on average have an income of £5,513 a year and spending of £6,897, they must be running up debts of around £1,400 a year over and above any student loans taken out.

The government-sponsored survey discussed above estimates that, by the end of a three-year course, the average student has debts from all sources of £8,666. The bulk of this (84 per cent) comprises student loans. Overdrafts account for around one-tenth and other commercial credit the rest. The government estimates that, with the introduction of variable top-up fees, the average debt could rise to £15,000 per student for those beginning their courses in 2006–7. This takes into account the financial help available for students from low-income backgrounds, so the figure may be a good deal higher if you are not eligible for such help.

CHAPTER 11

Insuring your possessions

Once you leave home, you need to think about protecting your belongings against loss, theft and damage. This applies not just when you set up your own permanent home, but even if you're off to live term-time in university halls of residence. Apart from taking steps to keep your belongings safe and secure, you could consider insurance.

> **Learning the hard way**
>
> A student is burgled every four minutes in Britain. According to the National Union of Students, the average student has over £4,000 worth of possessions. Home Office research in 1999 found that neighbourhoods dominated by students attract burglars because of poor security and rich pickings (for example, hi-fis, TVs and computers).

Who needs insurance?

Insuring your belongings is not compulsory. It's up to you to weigh up whether it is worth taking out cover. If you are lucky enough to have savings to fall back on, maybe you could replace all of your possessions out of your own resources if disaster struck. In that case, you might feel there is little point taking out insurance, especially if the cost were high. Or you might have possessions that are unique or of sentimental value and are therefore irreplaceable, in which case no insurance could help. But, for most people, losing all their possessions in, say, a fire, would be hard to manage and an insurance payout that enabled you to buy replacements would be very welcome.

What type of insurance do you need?

If you are buying a home or moving into unfurnished rental accommodation, choose house contents insurance. As well as personal possessions, it also covers furniture, carpets, and so on. If you live in a local authority or housing association property, ask the rent department whether it runs an insurance-with-rent scheme. Under such schemes, the local authority or housing association has negotiated a policy available to all its tenants, and instalment payments for the insurance will be collected along with rent payments. But check that the policy offers the cover you want (see below) and is competitively priced (see *Tips on shopping for insurance* on page 126).

When moving into furnished rented accommodation or student halls of residence, choose possessions insurance (also called belongings insurance). Several companies offer policies designed especially for students – see *Selection of companies offering student insurance*, below. Some student hall fees include basic cover for personal belongings, but you may need top-up belongings insurance, for example for your computer.

If you are a student, you may be tempted to rely on your parents' house contents insurance. However, an ordinary 'all-risks' extension, which covers possessions while outside the home, will not usually be adequate. Typically, it covers possessions away from home only for, say, a maximum of 60 days a year and may be restricted to certain types of belongings. However, some insurers do offer an extension to cover student sons and daughters away from home. If this applies with your policy, check carefully whether any exclusions apply that you would find it hard to comply with. For example, you might find that the insurer agrees cover only while your possessions are in your locked room. In practice, you may be carrying a laptop to lectures, lugging a bag around college, and so on. If a suitable extension is available, this will often be the cheapest way to get cover.

You may need separately to arrange cover for certain types of possessions, such as bicycles and musical instruments. Alternatively, cover might be included, but check whether there are any limits or exclusions with which you would be unhappy.

Selection of companies offering student insurance

- Endsleigh*
- Royal & SunAlliance (More Than)*
- Saxon*
- Bank of Scotland*
- HSBC*

What's covered?

A typical personal possessions policy would cover items against loss or damage caused by unpredictable events such as theft, fire, flood, burst pipes, and so on. There is no cover against normal wear and tear, and it is usually necessary to pay extra to add cover against damage caused accidentally (for example, because the item is dropped or a drink spilt over it). The policy terms and conditions will spell out precisely what is covered and in what circumstances, but typically the following are included:

- personal items such as clothes, books, TV, hi-fi equipment, CDs, videos, cameras, linen, soft furnishings, kitchen equipment, and so on. Student insurance normally covers possessions while in your student digs, at your parental home(s) and in transit between them
- loss of personal money, misuse of stolen credit cards
- computer equipment against theft. Consider paying extra for cover for accidental damage. Check whether cover is just for in your room(s) or also elsewhere
- extras (which might be included automatically or subject to an additional premium) might include:
  - loss of or damage to your landlord's property
  - loss of or damage to meters (for electricity, gas, and so on), library books and college property
  - personal liability (pays out if someone claims against you for injury to them or damage to their property)
  - lump sum paid on death of a parent or guardian on whom you were financially dependent
  - repayment of rent or accommodation fees paid in advance if you have to stop studying because of, say, illness or exam failure
  - repayment of student loan if you have to de-register from your course because of, say, illness or exam failure
  - cover for mobile phone
  - accidental damage to hi-fi, TV, DVD player, and so on
  - vacation top-up to cover items stored in student accommodation while you are back home during the holidays
  - deterioration of frozen foods due to a power cut
  - bicycles; also check whether the policy includes accidental damage cover
  - lump sum if you are injured by mugging, another assault or in a car accident
  - legal expenses insurance. This covers, for example, the cost of defending yourself if legal action is taken against you in connection with your home or possessions.

Choosing 'all risks' extends cover for specified items while they are outside your home and anywhere in the UK and sometimes abroad. Consider this, for example, to cover musical instruments and laptop computers.

A full-blown house contents insurance policy provides the cover described above and also covers your furniture, carpets, and so on. Fitted kitchens and bathroom fittings are usually covered by buildings insurance rather than contents insurance (see box below).

Buildings insurance

Buildings insurance covers loss or damage to the fabric of your home because of, for example, fire, storm, flooding, subsidence, and so on. If you live in rented accommodation, it is usually your landlord's responsibility to insure the building. If you are buying your own home with a mortgage, the lender will insist that you have adequate buildings insurance (whether taken out through the lender or arranged separately). If you own your own home outright, there is no compulsion to have buildings insurance, but generally you would be foolish not to have it. Most people could not afford to replace their home out of their own pocket if it burnt down, for example.

Excesses and exclusions

No insurance policy covers everything and possessions insurance is no exception. Therefore it is very important to read the small print setting out the full terms and conditions. Common limits and exclusions that you should watch out for are described below.

Excesses

An excess is the first part of a claim that you must pay out of your own pocket. For example, if your policy has a £50 excess and you are claiming £300, the most you'll get from the insurance is £300 − £50 = £250. You'll have to foot the bill for the other £50 yourself.

An excess may be compulsory (in other words, part of the terms you must accept as a condition of having the insurance), or voluntary, in which case you agree to pay the first part of any claim yourself in exchange for a reduction in the premium (see overleaf). Note also that different parts of the policy might have different amounts of compulsory excess.

Maximum sum insured

You choose this. In general, it should be the replacement cost of all your possessions – this is called a 'new-for-old' basis. It means that, if an item is lost or stolen, the insurance will pay out enough to replace it with a new one. So, when working out how much cover you need, you should add up the cost of buying all your possessions new.

Cover for just a few items is usually on an 'indemnity basis', meaning that the payout is reduced to allow for wear and tear. This typically applies to clothing and linen. It may also apply to bicycles, so check the policy wording carefully to ensure that you have the cover you need.

Single-item limit

The single-item limit is the maximum that can be claimed for any one item, even if its value is a lot higher. The limit could be reasonably high (say, £1,500), or surprisingly low (say, £150), so it is important to check your schedule carefully to see what limit applies to your particular policy. You must separately declare any items that are worth more than the single-item limit; the premium will normally be increased to extend full cover to these items.

The limit applies to collections as if each collection were a single item. Check the policy wording carefully for what counts as a collection. For example, the insurer is likely to treat all your CDs as a collection and similarly all your DVDs or computer games. So, if you had £1,000 worth of CDs and they were all stolen, you might find that the maximum you could claim was just £150, which would be far too little to replace them all.

Accidental damage cover

Even if you pay extra to add accidental damage cover to your policy, the cover might not apply to all your possessions. Common exclusions are contact lenses and bicycles. And some causes are also likely to be excluded, for example damage that occurs during cleaning or repair work.

All-risks cover

All risks extends cover to specified possessions when they are taken out of the home. But again, this does not mean every eventuality is covered. For example, it is common for there to be no cover if you leave the items unattended in a public place, and sports equipment is typically not covered if damage occurs while the equipment is in use. Your insurer might not be willing to extend cover at all to some vulnerable items, such as mobile phones.

How much does insurance cost?

What you pay (the 'premium') depends on a variety of factors, including:

- **level of cover** The higher the value of your possessions, the more you pay. But don't understate the value of your possessions – if you do, any claim you make may be scaled down proportionately, or could even be refused
- **where you live** Statistics show that, in some areas, theft is more common, and geographically some areas are more prone to flooding. Where a particular area is associated with more claims and/or more expensive claims, insurance will usually cost more
- **security** You may pay less if you have good locks on exit doors, window locks, a burglar alarm and/or belong to a neighbourhood watch
- **voluntary excess** You can get a reduction in your premium if you agree to meet the first part of any claim yourself. A voluntary excess is on top of any compulsory excess

- **how you pay** You will usually be charged extra if you choose to pay monthly rather than in a single lump sum. Conversely, some student policies let you pay in a single lump sum for three years' cover in return for a reduction in the total cost, but bear in mind that going for this option means you can't shop around each year for a better deal.

Cost of cover

Research by the National Union of Students found that on average students pay around £95 a year for possessions insurance.

Example

Arif is at Dundee University and shares a furnished rented flat just to the north of the city centre (an area classified by insurers as low risk). His most valuable possession is £1,200 worth of computer equipment, and his other belongings amount to £3,000. He obtains quotes for new-for-old personal possessions insurance, including all-risks cover for the computer. The quotes range from £95 to £185 for a year's cover.

Example

Arif's friend, George, goes to London University and lives in north London. He also has a £1,200 computer and £3,000 of other belongings and wants the same type of insurance as Arif. But George's quotes range from £200 to £250 a year, reflecting the higher-risk area in which he lives.

Choosing insurance

As the examples show, there can be a big difference in the price of insurance depending on the company you choose, so shop around. Try contacting one or two brokers for a quote. Many offer online quotation services either through their own websites or through link-ups with personal finance websites. To find a selection, type 'possessions insurance', 'student insurance' or 'house contents insurance' into a search engine like Google. If you prefer to shop around by phone, check out *Yellow Pages* or contact the British Insurance Brokers' Association (BIBA)★ for a list of local members.

Some insurers (called 'direct' companies) do not deal through brokers but only direct with the public. Other companies give you the option to deal direct or through a broker. These days, many insurers can provide quotes via the Internet if you want to deal this way.

Possessions insurance and house contents insurance policies run for one year at a time. Don't just renew with the same company each year – be prepared to shop around each time for a better deal. However, be aware that the cheapest policy will not necessarily be the best. You need to check also that it does offer the cover you want.

Tips on shopping for insurance

- Decide what type of insurance you need: possessions insurance or full house contents insurance.
- Decide what type of cover you want: basic only; accidental damage as well; all risks for some items?
- Work out the replacement value of your possessions. Note the value of any high-value items that might be more than a policy's single-item limit.
- Gather the other information you'll need, including your postcode, security arrangements such as window locks, type of door locks, make and model of valuable items, computers, mobile phones, and so on.
- Decide whether you would be happy to pay a voluntary excess and, if so, how much.
- Get quotes from two or three companies or one or two brokers (who will check out a panel of insurers for you).
- Ideally, before deciding to buy, get a copy of the full policy. Read the terms and conditions carefully. Check what exclusions, limits and compulsory excesses apply. Will all of your possessions be covered? Do you have some items over the valuables limit? Is cover outside the home included?
- If you have any queries or need extra cover, go back to the company or broker.

How to buy insurance

To get a quote, you must provide basic information about yourself, your possessions and your home. If you are happy with the price quoted, next take a look at the policy's terms and conditions to make sure you'll have the cover you want. If that's okay too, you can go ahead and buy.

At this stage, you fill in an application form (also called a 'proposal form'). This asks for similar information to that which you provided for the quote, but in greater detail. The answers you give on the proposal form will be part of your insurance contract with the company, so make sure the information you give is accurate. If a broker fills in the form for you, check the entries carefully.

If your application is accepted, you are usually covered immediately or, if later, from the date you specify. Within a few days, you usually receive a pack containing your full documents (see *The documents involved*, overleaf).

You usually have a choice of ways to pay, for example by credit card, debit card, cheque or direct debit. If you opt to pay, say, monthly by direct debit, you will usually pay a bit more than if you pay the full amount immediately as a single lump sum.

Your policy will run for a year, and 21 days before the end of the year you should normally receive a renewal notice inviting you to take out your cover for a further year. The offer will be on the basis of the answers you previously gave. You'll be given a summary of these, in order for you to check that they still apply. You should inform the insurer of any changes.

Your rights … your responsibilities

Duty to disclose material facts

Your possessions or home insurance policy is a contract between you and the insurance company. It is based on the information you supply and the policy terms and conditions. You are required to give the insurance company all 'material facts', that is, information which might influence the decision to insure you and at what price. The insurance company must make clear what information it needs by asking direct questions on the application form. You must answer the questions fully and honestly – if you don't, you could find any claims rejected.

The documents involved

Application form/Proposal form This is a questionnaire asking for information that the insurance company will use to decide whether to offer you cover and at what price.

Policy/Terms and conditions These are full details of what is covered and not covered by the policy. Typically, this is divided into sections for each type of cover. You will not necessarily be covered for all of the sections – it depends on what type of cover you have bought.

Schedule This is a summary of your cover, telling you, among other things, which sections of the policy apply and any special terms or exclusions.

This duty to disclose material facts does not apply just at the time you apply for insurance. If any changes occur during the policy year – for example, you move home or you make a major purchase which increases the value of your possessions substantially – you must tell the insurer.

Cancellation period

You have 14 days from the time the contract is concluded during which you can change your mind and back out of the policy with a full refund. This is useful if you've taken out cover but subsequently found a better deal or, as may happen if you bought by phone, you did not have chance to check the full terms and conditions before you bought.

Complaints

If you are unhappy about your dealings with an insurance company or broker, first contact the firm concerned.

If you are unhappy with the firm's response or it does not reply within a reasonable time (say, eight weeks), take your complaint to the appropriate independent complaints body. In the case of an insurance company, this is the Financial Ombudsman Service (FOS)★. In the case of most brokers and other insurance intermediaries, it will be the General Insurance Standards Council (GISC)★ until 14 January 2005, when the FOS will take over responsibility for these types of complaint as well.

Compensation

If your insurer should happen to go out of business, your premiums and any claims would, if appropriate, be covered by the Financial Services Compensation Scheme (FSCS)★. Compensation may cover the first £2,000 of your loss in full and 90 per cent of any additional amount.

CHAPTER 12

Car insurance

Reaching age 17 is a milestone because at last you can apply for a provisional licence and start learning to drive on the public highways. Driving lessons are fairly costly, but the real sting both while you are learning and as a new driver is car insurance.

Who needs car insurance?

Don't be tempted to skimp. This is one of the few areas where the law requires you to have insurance. You will be breaking the law if you drive on a road or other public place without at least a minimum of cover to pay out if you injure someone or damage his or her property.

Besides being irresponsible and anti-social, driving without insurance could lose you your licence and cost you up to £5,000 in fines. Although, under current rules, the fine might be only £200 for a first offence, the risk of losing your licence is very real. As standard, your licence will be endorsed with six to eight penalty points. During the first two years after passing your test, you are on probation and will lose your licence if you build up six or more points on it. You would go back to being a learner and have to take your test (including the theory part) all over again. Once the probationary period is over, you risk losing your licence for at least six months if you clock up 12 points in three years. In August 2003, the government announced a review of uninsured drivers with a view to increasing the penalties described above.

If you are driving someone else's car – for example, where a friend or family member takes you out for practice – both you and that person are jointly responsible for ensuring that you are insured to drive the particular car. You could either be covered by your own insurance or added to the other person's policy.

Driving practice

A person who sits with you to supervise your driving practice must be aged 21 or over and have held a full driving licence for at least three years. Unless this person is qualified as an instructor, he or she is not allowed to receive any payment from you (even for the petrol you use).

What is car insurance?

Car insurance is insurance that may pay out compensation if disaster strikes while you are driving or something happens to your car. There are three main types of policy.

Third party

This type of policy provides the minimum cover required by law. It covers claims against you if you have injured or killed someone, or damaged someone's property, while you are using your car. It also covers payments you may have to make to the National Health Service for emergency treatment.

The 'third parties' covered could include passengers travelling in your car, people in other vehicles, pedestrians, and so on. But third party cover does not pay out for your own injuries or any damage to your own car.

It would be unusual to take out just third party cover, but this is the type of cover you would have by default if, say, you drive someone else's car or you are relying on just a cover note (see page 139).

Third party fire and theft

This type of policy gives you the third party cover described above and, in addition, pays out if your own car is damaged or destroyed by fire, or the car is stolen or damaged following attempted theft.

Again, there is no payout for injuries sustained to yourself or for any damage to your car as a result of an accident. So this is usually appropriate insurance provided your car is not too valuable – worth less than, say, £3,000.

Comprehensive

With this type of policy, you get third party fire and theft insurance as described above and also cover for damage to your own car and its accessories as a result of an accident. The most that will be paid out for your car is its market value (its second-hand value) at the time it was lost or written off.

Often comprehensive policies come with a lot of add-ons as well, for example:

- **windscreen cover** Covers damage to your windscreen and other car windows

- **personal accident** Pays out specified lump sums if you die or suffer particular types of injury (such as loss of a limb) while using your car
- **medical expenses** Covers cost of treatment if you or anyone travelling with you is injured while using the car
- **personal effects** Covers property you are carrying in your car if it is lost or damaged because of fire or theft
- **replacement car** Provides a replacement while yours is off the road being repaired.

Excesses and exclusions

Commonly, car insurance policies come with 'excesses'. An excess is the first part of an insurance claim that is not covered and that you have to find out of your own pocket. For example, if you are claiming for £800 worth of damage and your policy has a £100 excess, the most you'll get back from your insurance is £800 − £100 = £700.

Excesses may be compulsory − in other words, part and parcel of the insurance, so you have no choice but to accept them if you want that particular policy. Alternatively, they may be voluntary, in which case you agree to the excess in return for a reduction in the cost of the insurance.

No insurance policy covers everything. The terms and conditions (see below) typically include detailed lists of risks, items and situations that are not covered. For example, a personal effects section usually will not cover valuables such as money, documents and tickets, and there's usually no theft cover if you leave your car unlocked and unattended.

How much will insurance cost?

The basic premium

Insurance companies work out what you pay (the 'premium') by estimating how much they might have to pay out to you in claims. This will depend on both the probability of your making a claim and the size of any likely claim. To make this estimate, the insurance company will ask you a lot of questions about:

- **you** The insurance company works out statistically how likely you are to claim given, for example, your sex, age, occupation, past record of accidents and convictions. Unfortunately, young people do on average tend to have more accidents than older people, so tend to be charged a lot more

- **where you use and keep the car** You'll pay more if you live in a busy urban area than in a remote rural one. This is not just because of the likelihood of more accidents, but also because the incidence of theft is so much higher in towns and cities. If you keep your car overnight in a locked garage, it's more secure so you'll usually pay less than if you keep it out on the street

- **the car** The insurance company risks paying out more if you drive a new or expensive car and statistics may suggest that people driving certain types of car (for example, sports cars) are more likely to make claims

- **who else drives the car** A policy can cover additional drivers, but you must tell the insurance company about them and it will assess the risk of that person causing a claim. As with 'you' above, the assessment will depend on sex, age, and so on. So, for example, if you are added to a parent's policy, your mum or dad will have to pay extra. Some companies vary the extra charge according to how often you'll be driving the car – e.g. everyday, just at week-ends or occasionally

- **the type of cover you want** Comprehensive costs more than third party fire and theft. If you want cover while driving on business, you may have to pay extra.

Example

Hannah is 17 and learning to drive. She lives in a small town in a largely rural area. Her mother, Jill, has offered to take Hannah out for practice. Currently, Jill pays £220 a year for comprehensive cover for her Volkswagen Polo. Adding Hannah to the insurance bumps the premium up to £540 a year.

Practice drives or more lessons?

Driving instructors agree that the more practice you can get while you are learning the better. But adding a young learner to a parent's or friend's insurance is costly. It could be more economical to buy extra lessons instead. Take the example of Hannah. Jill pays an extra £320 a year to add Hannah to her insurance. With driving lessons costing around £15 to £20 per hour in their area, for the same money Hannah could buy an extra 16 to 21 lessons with an instructor.

No claims bonus

It is standard practice with car insurance to give you a hefty premium reduction when you renew your cover if you have not made any claims in the recent past, a discount generally referred to as a no claims bonus. The longer your claim-free period, the bigger the reduction until the maximum is reached, which may range from, say, 60 to 75 per cent. The precise discounts vary from one insurer to another, but Table 12.1 shows a typical scale. If you switch insurer, your claim-free period can be transferred to the new company.

Of course, new drivers have not had a chance to build up their no claims bonus beyond the starting rate, which is another reason why your premium is likely to be higher than for an older driver.

Usually, you lose some no claims bonus at renewal if you have made one or more claims in the past year. Typically, you move back two steps on the scale. Your discount continues to be lower in subsequent years until you have built up the maximum discount – see the example below. You need to weigh up the total discount you would lose against what you would gain by claiming. If your claim would be fairly small, it may be better to foot the bill yourself and keep the discount.

Once you have several years' discount, you can often protect it by paying an extra premium. In that case, you do not lose any discount if you make just one claim during the year.

Table 12.1 Example of a no claims bonus scale

After this many years without a claim	Your premium at renewal is reduced by this much	If you make one claim, your discount at renewal is reduced to
0	0%	0%
1	30%	0%
2	40%	0%
3	50%	30%
4 or more	60%	40%

Excesses

You can usually get a reduction in the basic premium if you agree to a voluntary excess (see above). The larger the excess, the bigger the premium reduction. It is always worth going for an excess that matches the amount you would be unwilling to claim because of the effect on your no claims bonus (see the example opposite).

Choosing insurance

If you are driving a fairly old car, third party fire and theft cover will probably be adequate and will save you money. If your car is worth more than, say, £3,000, consider comprehensive cover.

Different insurers specialise in different types of business, so there can be a huge variation in premiums from one company to another. Therefore, you should definitely shop around. The easiest way to do this is to contact one or two brokers for a quote. Many offer online quotation services either through their own websites or through link-ups with personal finance websites. To find a selection, type 'car insurance' into a search engine like Google. If you prefer to shop around by phone, check out *Yellow Pages* or contact the British Insurance Brokers' Association (BIBA)★ for a list of local members.

Some insurers (called 'direct' companies) do not deal through brokers but only direct with the public. Other companies give you the option to deal direct or through a broker. These days, many insurers can provide quotes via the Internet if you want to deal this way.

Example

Jerry's basic insurance premium is likely to be about £660 at renewal. His insurer uses the no claims bonus scale in Table 12.1, and provided Jerry doesn't make a claim this year, he'll get a 40 per cent discount at renewal, reducing his premium to (100% – 40%) × £660 = £396. However, Jerry misjudges a pinchpoint and damages his car's bodywork. The cost of the repairs comes to £430. He could claim this on his insurance, but he would then lose all his no claims bonus and get a reduced discount for the next few years. The lost discount (see Table 12.2) comes to more than the amount he could claim, so it is not worth claiming. Given the amount of discount involved, Jerry might as well agree to a voluntary excess up to around £600 if this would earn him a reduction in his annual premium.

12.2 Difference between making a claim or not

Year	If Jerry does not claim		If Jerry does claim		No claims bonus lost as a result of claiming*
	Jerry's no claims bonus	Jerry's premium*	Jerry's no claims bonus	Jerry's premium*	
At next renewal	40%	£396	nil	£660	£264
First year after	50%	£330	30%	£462	£132
Second year after	60%	£264	40%	£396	£132
Third year after	60%	£264	50%	£330	£66
Fourth year after	60%	£264	60%	£264	£0
Total no claims bonus lost					**£594**

* Ignores any general change in premiums from year to year.

A car insurance policy runs for one year at a time. Don't just renew with the same company each year – be prepared to shop around each time for a better deal. However, be aware that the cheapest policy will not necessarily be the best. You need to check also that it does offer the cover you want.

At the time of writing, a few firms had a good reputation for offering competitive deals to younger drivers and so could be worth checking out. They included Endsleigh★, Tesco★ and Direct Choice★.

How to buy insurance

To obtain a quote, you must provide basic information about yourself and your car. If you are happy with the price quoted, next take a look at the policy's terms and conditions to make sure you'll have the cover you want. If that's okay too, you can go ahead and buy.

At this stage, you fill in an application form (also called a 'proposal form'). This asks for similar information to that which you provided for the quote, but in greater detail. The answers you give on the proposal form will be part of your insurance contract with the company, so make sure the information you give is accurate. If a broker fills in the form for you, check the entries carefully.

If your application is accepted, you are usually covered immediately or, if later, from the date you specify. A cover note is usually issued straight away, which is your temporary proof that you have at least the minimum cover required by law. Within a few days, you usually receive a pack containing your full documents (see *The documents involved*, opposite).

You usually have a choice of ways to pay, for example by credit card, debit card, cheque or direct debit. If you opt to pay, say, monthly by direct debit, you will usually pay more than if you pay the full amount immediately as a single lump sum. This is because you are basically taking out a loan to spread the payments.

Your policy will run for a year, and 21 days before the end of the year you should normally receive a renewal notice inviting you to take out your cover for a further year. The offer will be on the basis of the answers you previously gave. You'll be given a summary of these, in order for you to check that they still apply. You should inform the insurer of any changes.

The documents involved

Application form/Proposal form This is a questionnaire asking for information which the insurance company will use to decide whether to offer you cover and at what price.

Policy/Terms and conditions These are full details of what is covered and not covered by the policy. Typically, this is divided into sections for each type of cover. You will not necessarily be covered for all the sections – it depends what type of cover you have bought.

Schedule This is a summary of your cover, telling you among other things which sections of the policy apply, any special terms or exclusions and who is covered (for example, just you or you and other named drivers).

Cover note A temporary record of your cover incorporating a temporary certificate to say that you have the minimum cover required by law.

Certificate of insurance Proof that you have the minimum insurance required by law. This is the document you may need to produce for the police. You will also need to produce this in order to purchase vehicle excise duty ('car tax').

Your rights ... your responsibilities

Duty to disclose material facts

Car insurance is a contract between you and the insurance company. It is based on the information you supply and the policy's terms and conditions. You are required to give the insurance company all 'material facts', that is, information which might influence the decision to insure you and at what price. The insurance company must make clear what information it needs by asking direct questions on the application form. You must answer the questions fully and honestly – if you don't, you could find any claims rejected.

This duty to disclose material facts does not apply just at the time you apply for insurance. If any changes occur during the policy year – for example, you move house, receive a driving conviction or want to add another driver to the policy – you must tell the insurer.

Cancellation period

You have 14 days from the time the contract is concluded during which you can change your mind and back out of the policy with a full refund. This is useful if you've taken out cover but subsequently found a better deal or, as may happen if you bought by phone, you did not have chance to check the full terms and conditions before you bought.

Complaints

If you are unhappy about your dealings with an insurance company or broker, first contact the firm concerned.

If you are unhappy with the firm's response or it does not reply within a reasonable time (say, eight weeks), take your complaint to the appropriate independent complaints body. In the case of an insurance company, this is the Financial Ombudsman Service (FOS)★. In the case of most brokers and other insurance intermediaries, it will be the General Insurance Standards Council (GISC)★ until 14 January 2005, when the FOS will take over responsibility for these types of complaints as well.

Compensation

If your insurer should happen to go out of business, your premiums and any claims would, if appropriate, be covered in full by the Financial Services Compensation Scheme (FSCS)★, so you should not lose out.

CHAPTER 13

Holiday money

If you are going on holiday abroad, you'll need some foreign currency to spend. There are three main ways to take money with you: cash, traveller's cheques or plastic. In part, which you take with you depends on:

- how much you want to take
- where you are going, and
- your attitude towards risk.

But, usually, it is best to take a combination of all three. Table 13.1 summarises the main pros and cons of each.

Table 13.1 Ways to take money abroad

	Cash foreign currency	Traveller's cheques	Plastic Credit cards	Debit/ cash cards
Widely accepted in cities etc.	Yes	Yes	Usually yes	Usually yes
Widely accepted in other areas	Yes	Often no	Often no	Often
Use immediately	Yes	Usually no	Not necessarily	Not necessarily
Safe: can be traced/stopped if lost or stolen	No	Yes	Yes	Yes
Quickly replaced if lost or stolen	No	Yes	No	No
Can travel without planning how much money you'll need	No	No	Yes	Yes

Cash (foreign currency)

How do you use it?

Pay direct for whatever you buy.

Where is it accepted?

Virtually everywhere, but in some places hard currencies (see page 150) may be preferred to the local currency. It may be difficult to spend large notes, so make sure when you buy your currency that you ask for at least some smaller denomination notes. It's useful to have a few coins, for example for toilet stops and parking machines. Since bureaux de change and other outlets usually do not supply coins, get into the habit of keeping some back for use on future trips or ask friends and family if they have any (which you can replace on your return).

Change for the better

Keep a few coins for your next trip, but consider donating surplus foreign coins and notes to charity. A survey for Age Concern estimated that British households have roughly £95 million of leftover foreign currency lying around at home.

Immediacy

Cash is the only form of travel money you can be sure of being able to use straight away. Therefore, take at least some cash even if only to pay for refreshments, transport to your hotel, and so on.

Risk

Unfortunately, cash is the most insecure form of travel money. If lost or stolen, it can't be traced. Travel insurance policies usually cover lost or stolen cash only up to a limit – say, £250 or £500 – and the cash will not normally be replaced immediately.

WHEN THEY SAID PUT IT IN THE HOTEL SAFE, THEY DIDN'T MEAN BRING THE SAFE WITH YOU.

Cost

You pay in one or more of these ways:

- **exchange rate** The 'spread' between the rate at which you buy and the rate at which you sell is a cost (see *What do you get for your money?*, overleaf). In addition, exchange rates vary from one provider to another. The lower the exchange rate when you buy foreign currency, the more you are paying

- **commission** This is a fee you pay to whoever sells you the currency and it varies from one provider to another. It is usually a percentage of the amount of money you are changing, say, 1 per cent to 2 per cent of the transaction. There may be a minimum commission of, for example, £3 to £5

- **flat fee** Instead of commission, some providers charge a flat fee – for example £5 – regardless of the size of the transaction.

Some providers do not charge any commission at all, but a 'commission-free' deal is not necessarily cheap. Check whether the exchange rate is competitive and whether there is a flat fee instead. A minimum commission or flat fee is often expensive if you are changing only a small amount. However, a flat fee can be good value if you are changing a large sum.

If you convert foreign currency back into sterling, you may have to pay commission or a fee again, though if you go back to the same provider they may waive this. However, you'll pay the exchange rate spread. And you may make a loss or gain if exchange rates have changed since you bought the currency.

Which? surveys suggest that the savings through shopping around for foreign currency are modest – say, £5 on a transaction of around £100. Airports and ports are not necessarily more expensive than other providers. But watch out for special deals – for example, your own bank might have a special deal for student customers.

What do you get for your money?

The exchange rate tells you how much foreign currency you get for each pound, or how many pounds you get for each unit of foreign currency.

Most exchange rates are not fixed and move up and down all the time. To get an idea of the current rate, check in newspapers, on the Internet, on television text services, and so on. If you have access to the Internet, you can convert one currency to another using a currency converter, such as www.xe.net/ucc.

The published rate and the rate used in currency converters is usually the 'mid-rate'. This is halfway between a lower rate at which you can buy and the higher rate at which you sell. The difference between these – the 'spread' – is, in effect, a charge you pay that goes to the dealer supplying or accepting the currency.

Example

Nat converts £100 into euros. She is quoted a buying rate of €1.3644. This means she gets €1.3644 for each £1, a total of €136.44. At the same time, Chris converts €136.44 into pounds and is quoted a selling rate of €1.4271. This means he must pay €1.4271 for each £1, so he gets €136.44/€1.4271 = £95.61. The difference between the buying and selling rates of €1.4271 − €1.3644 = €0.0627 is the spread and this creates the charge of £100 − £95.61 = £4.39 that Nat and Chris in effect pay between them.

Where do you get it?

Banks, some building societies, bureaux de change (independent, at airports, ports, through travel agents), the Post Office, financial arms of some supermarkets, and so on.

Scottish notes

In most countries, the local currency is issued only by that country's central bank. The UK is unusual because its central bank, the Bank of England, is not the only note issuer. A few private banks in Scotland and Northern Ireland are also allowed to issue notes. These have exactly the same value as Bank of England notes.

Notes issued by Scottish banks are accepted anywhere within Scotland and are generally accepted in the rest of the UK. But Scottish notes are unlikely to be accepted if you try to use them abroad, such as to buy foreign currency, so take Bank of England notes instead.

How do you get it?

In person at a branch. Alternatively, order by phone or the Internet – often currency can be delivered to your home (there may be an extra charge, for example £5), otherwise you pick it up at a local branch. You can either get your foreign currency before you go or take pounds with you and change them once you arrive at your destination. Usually it's cheaper to change money before you go.

You can often buy common currencies straight away over the counter, but more unusual currencies may have to be ordered, which could take several days. Branches on university campuses often hold a wider range of currencies.

Traveller's cheques

How do you use them?

Traveller's cheques can be denominated in sterling or a foreign currency. You convert the cheques into cash at a bank or bureau de change abroad, or in some places they can be used direct to pay for things, for example, hotel or restaurant bills.

Traveller's cheques have space for two signatures. When you first pick them up, you sign each cheque in the first space, leaving the second blank. When you use or cash the cheque, you sign the second space in the presence of the bank or person you are paying.

Where are they accepted?

They are widely accepted in cities, larger towns and main tourist areas, but can be difficult to use in rural areas and some countries, such as China. Sterling traveller's cheques are accepted in many countries, but in the USA, South America and some other areas, dollar cheques are more useful.

Immediacy

In cities, larger towns and main tourist areas, traveller's cheques may be accepted direct to pay bills in hotels, restaurants and some other outlets. In the USA, dollar traveller's cheques are very widely accepted in this way. But otherwise, you first need to exchange the cheques for cash at a bank or bureau de change – this can be a problem if you need cash outside banking hours, at weekends, on a public holiday or you are in a remote area with no banks.

Risk

Traveller's cheques are the most secure form of travel money. Each cheque is numbered. Make sure you have a record of the numbers. If the cheques are lost or stolen, you call an emergency helpline, giving the numbers of the cheques. They will then be refunded. Usually, replacement cheques can be delivered to you within a day or so.

Cost

In effect you pay through the exchange rate spread each time you switch currency (see *What do you get for your money?*, on page 144), so, for example, if you take dollar traveller's cheques which you then exchange for a local currency, you'll lose twice on exchange rates – once on the switch from sterling to dollars and again on the switch from dollars to the local currency.

There are also fees to pay. You are normally charged commission when you buy the cheques (say, 1 per cent with a minimum of £3). When you cash them at a foreign bank or use them to pay for something abroad, you may have to pay commission again; you should also check that the exchange rate you get is competitive.

You can often convert unused traveller's cheques back to sterling at no extra charge. With foreign currency cheques, you may make a loss or gain if exchange rates have changed since you bought the currency.

If you buy online or by phone, you may also have to pay a delivery charge. Shop around for a good deal.

Where do you get them?

Banks, some building societies, bureaux de change, the Post Office, financial arms of some supermarkets, and so on.

How do you get them?

In person at a branch. Alternatively, order by phone or via the Internet, in which case they can often be delivered to your home (though there may be an extra charge, perhaps £5), or you pick them up at a local branch.

Debit and credit cards

How do you use them?

Just as you would at home, use your cards abroad to get foreign currency from a cash machine or to pay direct for something in the local currency. Most ATMs will either automatically recognise the origin of your card and switch to instructions in English or have an option that lets you select English. In other respects, use ATMs just as you would in the UK.

In shops, hotels, and so on, use cards for payment as you would in the UK. In France, you may be asked to key your PIN into a pad instead of signing a slip. Although this system is due to be introduced throughout the UK from 2005, the French system is not compatible with UK cards. Try saying: '*Les cartes Britanniques ne sont pas des cartes à puce, mais à pistes magnétiques. Ma carte est valable et je vous serais reconnaissant d'en demander la confirmation auprès de votre banque ou de votre centre de traitement.*' ('British cards do not contain microchips, but have magnetic strips. My card is valid and I would be grateful if you would request authorisation from your bank or processing centre.')

Where are they accepted?

Plastic cards are widely accepted in cities, larger towns and main tourist areas. They might not be accepted in remoter areas or some countries, so check before you travel.

Immediacy

Provided plastic is accepted, your cards can be used to pay all kinds of bills, but they are not normally accepted for very small transactions, so make sure you have some cash as well. They can be used in ATMs to obtain cash, which is handy with debit cards and cash cards, but not advisable in the case of credit cards since there is an extra charge for cash withdrawals (see below).

Risk

Cards can be stopped if lost or stolen and your liability for misuse by a fraudster or thief is capped at £50 (and in practice is usually nothing). In the event of loss or theft, phone the emergency helpline immediately. Although your cards can be replaced, this usually takes some time. However, if you have joined a card protection scheme, it may well include a means by which to get cash to you in an emergency.

Guard yourself against fraud, such as skimming, when paying by plastic. See Chapters 2 and 5 for tips on looking after your cards.

Cost

The card issuer converts the transaction into sterling at the exchange rate on the day that details reach your account (not the day you make the transaction). Because card issuers combine your transaction with lots of others, usually the exchange rate is competitive. However, most card issuers add an 'exchange-rate loading' – typically 1.75 per cent to 2.75 per cent of the amount of the transaction – so check your card's terms and conditions before you use it abroad.

If you use a credit card or some debit cards to get foreign currency from a cash machine or to pay for currency at a bank or bureau de change, this will be treated as a cash withdrawal and the normal cash advance fee – typically 1.5 per cent to 2 per cent of the amount withdrawn – will be charged, even if you pay off your next bill in full. Check the terms and conditions applying to your card.

You also incur your normal card charges. So you'll pay interest if you do not pay off your full credit-card balance, and will also pay interest and maybe other charges if using your debit card or cash card makes you go overdrawn.

Where do you get them?

Debit and cash cards are a standard feature of current accounts and many basic bank accounts – see Chapter 1. Credit cards are issued by banks and a wide range of other providers – see Chapter 5.

Which currency should you take with you?

In general, for cash, you should take the local currency of the country you are visiting. Many popular holiday destinations now use the euro (see *Countries which use the euro*, below).

Countries which use the euro

The following countries use the euro:

- in the European Union (EU): Austria, Belgium, Finland, France, Germany, Greece, Italy, Luxembourg, The Netherlands, Portugal, Republic of Ireland, Spain
- Andorra, Monaco, San Marino, Vatican City
- some overseas territories of EU countries, such as the Azores, Balearic Islands, Canary Islands, Guadeloupe, Guyana, Madeira and Martinique.

In some regions, it is better to take a hard currency rather than local money. A 'hard currency' is one in which there is widespread confidence, so it is widely traded and accepted. The main hard currencies are the dollar, sterling and the euro. In many countries, hard currencies (as cash or traveller's cheques) are accepted either as well as local currency or sometimes in preference to local currency – for example, the dollar is widely accepted throughout South America.

Be aware that some countries put restrictions on the amount of currency you can bring into or take out of the country. The bank, bureau de change or other provider should be able to advise you on the best currencies to take as cash and traveller's cheques and any restrictions that apply. A good source of information if you have access to the Internet is *www.travel-guide.com*.

How much money should you take with you?

How much foreign currency you need depends on personal factors, such as how much you can afford to spend and how long you will be abroad. Additionally, some countries put limits on the amount of local and/or foreign currency that can either be brought into a country or taken out again.

Consider limiting the amount you have in cash at any one time to the sum covered by your travel insurance (typically £250 or £500). Take enough money in total to cover emergencies as well as your planned spending. If using a debit card, consider asking your bank to agree an overdraft facility so that you can draw enough cash out in an emergency. If relying on a credit card, consider asking for a temporary higher credit limit so that you'll have enough available in an emergency.

Holiday money checklist

- Don't rely on one form of money – take a mix of cash, traveller's cheques and cards.
- Check with a foreign-exchange provider, for both cash and traveller's cheques, which currencies are best for the country you are going to. Check with your card issuer whether credit and debit cards are accepted in that country.
- Shop around for foreign currency and traveller's cheques – remember to check whether the exchange rate is competitive as well as the commission charge.
- Where possible, choose sterling traveller's cheques because unused ones can usually be paid back into your account at no charge.
- Take enough money in total to cover emergencies as well as planned spending.
- Consider limiting cash to the amount covered by your travel insurance.
- Check the expiry date on plastic cards before you travel and, if necessary, get updated cards.
- Consider asking for a higher credit limit (credit card) or overdraft (debit card) in case you need extra to cover emergencies.
- If possible, take more than one type of card with you, so that if one does not work in some cash machines there is a chance the other might.

Beware; be safe

Tourists are likely to be carrying money and other valuables. They also often lack awareness of which areas are dodgy, and may be handicapped by a poor grasp of the language. So, when you are travelling, you are likely to be a target for scams and crime. Therefore, you should be on your guard. Here is a rundown of some of the ploys to which you might be prey.

Black-market bargain

In some countries – especially within Eastern Europe, Africa and South America – there is a flourishing black market where you can get currency commission-free. But make sure you're not conned.

A common trick is as follows: you hand over, say, sterling or dollars. In return, you receive a huge wodge of local currency. You are warned to stash it away quickly so as not to attract thieves. When you get back to your hotel, you check the stash of cash to find:

- you have been given low-denomination notes that come to too little
- you have been given worthless notes – perhaps old currency, or
- you have a few good notes on the outside, but most of the wodge is made up of cut-to-size newspaper.

Bogus official

You find yourself in the company of a fellow traveller and get chatting. A police officer or other official, comes up and explains that he or she is on the trail of fake banknotes. The police officer asks to see your passport and money. The fellow tourist produces his or hers first, the officer checks the documents and cash and hands them back. Your turn. You hand over your money and papers. The officer and fellow traveller (who was of course part of the scam) do a runner, taking your cash with them.

Tricky taxi

This is allegedly a common trick in the USA, especially New York. It only works with dollars and is usually played just after you arrive at the airport. You get into a taxi and as you near your destination, you offer up a $100 bill in payment. The driver says you have given him too little and holds up the $1 bill you have apparently handed him – an understandable mistake, of course, since you are a stranger newly arrived, tired and all the notes look the same. Of course, by sleight of hand the driver has pocketed your $100 and substituted the $1. Make sure you use only metered taxis and try to pay the correct amount instead of handing over large notes.

Skimming

You use your credit card to pay for, say, a meal in a restaurant. Later, when your holiday is over, you find unexplained bills charged to your account. Chances are you have been a victim of skimming. When you made a genuine transaction, your card was also swiped through a fraudster's machine which copied the details carried on the card's magnetic stripe. These were used to make a fake card. The fraudster then went shopping with the counterfeit card and the transactions turn up on your credit-card statement. Skimming typically happens in places like restaurants, bars, hotels and petrol stations, where your card may be briefly out of your sight. However, you should not be liable for these fraudulent transactions. Under the Consumer Credit Act 1974, you are not liable for any loss due to misuse of your card details while your card remains in your possession.

Sickly distraction

In one of the latest tricks from South America, someone will be sick on you and in the commotion you'll find your bag is stolen. All sorts of other 'distractions' are used in a similar way: someone accuses you of sitting in his or her seat while an accomplice steals your bag; someone stops abruptly in front of you to deal with his or her child while the person behind lifts valuables from your pocket; at the airport someone just ahead of you sets off the security gate after your hand baggage has gone through the X-ray machine while an accomplice on the other side walks off with your baggage.

Keep your money safe

- If you carry a bag, wear it strapped across you with fastenings towards you.
- Use a money belt or secure inside pocket.
- Look after handbags and jackets – for example, don't hang them on the back of a chair where they could be vulnerable to pickpockets.
- While driving, keep bags and valuables out of sight, especially in slow-moving traffic. Opportunist thieves may open a door and snatch anything tempting.
- Don't keep your cash, traveller's cheques, cards and passport together in case they get lost or stolen.
- If possible, store cash you do not need immediately in a hotel safe.
- Sign traveller's cheques as soon as you get them (but do not countersign until you use or cash them).
- Write down the serial numbers of traveller's cheques, your credit- and debit-card numbers and expiry dates (but not your PINs), and the emergency phone numbers to call if they are lost or stolen. Keep this record separate from the cheques and cards.
- Only carry around one card at a time – leave the other in a hotel safe – to reduce the risk of losing them all.
- When paying by card, do not let the card out of your sight.
- Consider joining a card protection scheme – this makes it easier to cancel lost or stolen cards and often includes arrangements to send you cash in an emergency.

CHAPTER 14

Travel insurance

Whether you're going on a short holiday, taking a gap year or backpacking around the world, one of the essentials to take with you is a good travel insurance policy.

Who needs travel insurance?

When planning a trip or travelling, there is always a risk of running into problems that can be very costly, for example:

- it's standard to pay for accommodation, travel, and so on up front. If you have to cancel, you want to be sure you can get your money back quickly and in full
- if you fall ill, the cost of treatment abroad or of flying you home could run to many thousands of pounds. Around one in three travel insurance claims are due to medical problems
- if you accidentally injure someone or damage his or her property, you could face a hefty payment for damages
- you might need to replace personal belongings that have been lost or stolen.

Travel insurance is designed to ensure that you are not out of pocket in the sort of situations described above.

In general terms, it is not compulsory for you to have travel insurance. However, tour operators can insist that you do have cover for particular holidays or activities. In that case, the requirement to have insurance must be made clear and the tour operator must tell you about any suitable cover it can offer; however, you cannot be forced to take out the tour operator's own insurance. In most cases, you will do much better to shop around for your own policy.

In practice, tour operators sometimes make it very difficult for you to exercise your right to shop around. It is common practice for operators and travel agents to refuse to confirm your holiday booking until you show evidence of adequate travel insurance. So, if you have not arranged cover in advance, you may risk losing a particular holiday or special deal. In that situation, many people panic, grin and bear the high cost, and sign up for the tour operator's own insurance after all.

The moral is: plan ahead. If you're travelling abroad, you really would be foolish to go without travel insurance, but fix up a good policy *before* you book the holiday.

If you're travelling in the UK, you probably do not need a travel policy. Health problems will be covered by the NHS, and if you have an 'all-risks' extension to your possessions or house contents insurance (see Chapter 11), you'll be covered in the event of theft. But if, say, you're staying in rented accommodation, you might want insurance to cover you against damaging the property or its contents. And if you'll be taking part in adventurous activities or sports, taking out suitable insurance would be wise.

All of the above applies equally to school trips. If you'll be going abroad or on an activity trip, insurance is sensible. The school might offer to arrange cover, but you do not have to take up the policy chosen by the school. You can instead arrange your own insurance. If you are already included on insurance arranged by your parents, check that the policy covers you while travelling independently from your family.

Isn't an E111 enough?

An E111 is a form that entitles you to state-provided emergency medical treatment in countries that are members of the European Economic Area (EEA) – see Table 14.1. You receive treatment on the same terms as nationals of the country concerned and the treatment will be either free or provided at reduced cost. If you have had to pay something, you can usually claim a full or partial refund from the authorities of the country that you visited. An E111 does not normally cover private treatment.

An E111 is not a substitute for travel insurance because it covers only emergency treatment and there is no non-medical cover – for example, for personal liability or your baggage. So you still need proper travel insurance. However, it is often a term of travel insurance that, if you use your E111, your insurer will waive the excess that would normally apply to a medical claim (see below).

To obtain an E111, get leaflet T5 *Health advice for travellers* available from Post Offices and travel agents. Fill in the form on the back of the leaflet and take it to a Post Office. The Post Office will stamp and sign the form for you. The E111 is free and is valid indefinitely. When you use it abroad, you will need to hand it over or provide a copy, so it's a good idea to travel with at least one photocopy. If you have to hand over the original, get a new E111 when you return to the UK.

   Outside the EEA, the UK has reciprocal healthcare arrangements with some countries, enabling you to obtain emergency
state treatment on the same basis as nationals. You may have to
pay for this treatment and payment cannot usually be reclaimed.

   There are many countries with which the UK has no reciprocal agreement at all – see Table 14.1. You will have to pay for
treatment and the cost may be high. Make sure you have travel
insurance to cover medical costs that can't be reclaimed.

Table 14.1 Getting emergency medical treatment abroad

Countries where you can use your E111	Austria
	Belgium
	Denmark
	Finland
	France
	Germany
	Greece
	Iceland
	Ireland
	Italy
	Liechtenstein
	Luxembourg
	Netherlands
	Norway
	Portugal
	Spain
	Sweden
Examples of countries with which the UK has no reciprocal agreement	All African countries
	All of Asia
	Canada
	Most Caribbean islands
	Cyprus
	All Middle Eastern countries
	All of the Pacific region except Australia and New Zealand
	All South American nations
	Switzerland
	Turkey
	USA and Mexico

What type of insurance do you need?

If you travel infrequently, you could just take out single-trip insurance as and when you need it. But, if you go away more than twice a year, you'll probably save money by taking out an annual multi-trip policy.

An annual policy typically covers any number of trips during the year provided each one lasts no more than a specified length of time – say, 31 days. Most annual policies automatically include about two weeks' winter sports cover a year.

If you are going away for longer than a month – for example, during a gap year – you'll need long-stay insurance. Some policies are aimed specifically at backpackers and tend to have extra cover thrown in, such as a payout if you are the victim of a mugging.

Standard policies generally exclude cover for risky sports, such as scuba diving or snowboarding, so you'll need a specialist sports or winter sports policy. Most providers offer a winter sports version of their policy. A few providers specialise in cover for other sports as well.

What's covered?

Cover varies from one policy to another, but Table 14.2 sets out the core elements you should expect and the level of cover you should normally aim to have.

Medical emergency

In general, £2 million of medical cover should be ample, so do not be overly impressed by 'Rolls Royce' policies that charge extra for, say, £5 million or £10 million of cover.

Baggage

Unlike possessions insurance (see Chapter 11), with most policies the baggage section usually covers your possessions only up to their second-hand value, not on a new-for-old basis.

Table 14.2 Summary of the minimum travel cover you should normally have

Type of cover	Minimum recommended
Cancellation of your holiday or cutting it short (curtailment)	Full cost of the holiday
Medical emergency	£2 million
Personal liability (for injury you cause to someone else or damage to someone else's possessions)	£2 million
Baggage	Value of your belongings – £1,500 is usually enough (watch single item/valuable item limit, e.g. £150 or £300)
Personal money (cash, traveller's cheques, etc.)	Often £250 – £500
Loss of passport	£250

If you have an all-risks extension (see page 122) to your possessions or house contents insurance, your baggage may already be covered while away from home. Given that cover under this policy, apart from that for clothing, will almost certainly be new-for-old, you may prefer to rely on this insurance rather than a travel policy.

Some travel insurance policies give you the option to cancel the baggage coverage in return for a cost saving. This is worth doing if you are sure you already have cover through your possessions or contents insurance.

If you are relying on the baggage section of your travel insurance, be aware that there is usually a single item/valuable item limit on possessions. If you'll be taking something more valuable with you – say, an expensive camera – see if you can pay extra to increase the cover. Alternatively, consider extending your house contents or possessions insurance to cover the item while you are away.

Sports cover

Don't assume that a standard travel policy will cover any sports equipment you take with you. A specialist sports policy will cover equipment, but check what limits and conditions apply, for example:

- a limit on the maximum that will be paid out even if your equipment is worth more
- a reduction in cover according to the age of the equipment
- special conditions about looking after the equipment – for example, a requirement that you use ski locks if your skis are to be left unattended, say in a rack outside a restaurant.

If you are taking part in dangerous sports, make sure that the medical cover includes the cost of search-and-rescue operations should you need them – for example, to get you off a mountain after a climbing or skiing accident.

Extras

As well as the core cover shown in Table 14.2, many policies include other areas of cover, such as legal expenses (for example, up to £10,000), hospital benefit (for example, up to £10 for each day you are hospitalised), and travel delay (for example, £10 for each 12-hour delay).

Most policies have an emergency helpline for you to call for advice if something goes wrong while you are abroad.

Excesses and exclusions

Most travel insurance is not tailored to the individual. Instead, you buy a one-size-fits-all policy and the insurance company controls its costs by putting exclusions on the claims it will meet. Therefore, it is very important that you check the policy exclusions before you buy to see how they might apply to you.

The most important exclusion usually concerns health problems. Standard travel insurance does not pay out for claims related to a health problem which existed at the time you bought the policy – called a 'pre-existing condition' – unless you declared the problem and the insurer agreed to cover it. A pre-existing health problem includes such common complaints as asthma even if they are well managed so, if in doubt, declare the condition.

The health exclusion usually also extends to anyone whose health would affect your travel plans. For example, if a close relative was already severely ill when you bought the insurance, the policy would normally not pay out if you subsequently cancelled your holiday because that person had become worse or had died.

There are limits on each section of the policy. You should make sure the limits are high enough given your own circumstances. For example, a policy that limited the payout to £1,000 if you cancelled the holiday would not be enough if the holiday cost you £1,500.

Usually, there is a policy excess for each section. An excess is the first part of a claim that you must pay yourself. For example, if you claim back medical emergency costs of £1,200, you might have to pay the first £100 yourself, reducing the amount you get from the insurance company to £1,100. Many insurers waive the medical excess if you make a claim having used your E111.

Check what conditions apply for a claim to be valid. For example, sports equipment may need to be locked up when not in use and, if something is stolen, you must usually have reported the theft to the local police. If you have a medical emergency, it is usually a condition that you call the emergency helpline either before or as soon as possible after starting to receive treatment.

Cost

What you pay for travel insurance (the premium) will depend mainly on:

- **where you are going** Usually there are different premiums for the UK, Europe, Rest of the World excluding USA, and Worldwide. The more countries are covered, the more you pay

- **how long you are going for** The longer you are away, the higher the premium
- **whether you want cover for sports** Including winter sports or other 'dangerous' sports usually costs extra.

If you are likely to go on holiday more than twice a year, it is usually cheaper to buy an annual multi-trip policy rather than separate cover for each trip.

Shop around to find a good deal. Phone and Internet companies tend to be the cheapest – get quotes from three or four. Bear in mind that cheap is not the same as value for money – check the cover as well as the price.

If you have all-risks possessions or house contents (or possessions) insurance, see if you can cancel the baggage section of the travel policy for a premium saving. Expect to save 10 to 20 per cent.

Table 14.3 Examples of the cost of annual travel insurance policies versus a single-trip policy

Company	Premium for a single person (age 18–64) for a European holiday	
	Annual policy	Single-trip policy for two weeks
Direct Travel	£31.00	£11.00
Journeywise	£39.25	£15.25
Options	£30.45	£10.45
Leading Edge	£49.00	£12.00

Premiums correct in January 2004.

When to buy insurance

Buying travel cover at the same time as you book a holiday makes life easy, but you'll pay for the convenience (see below). An important feature of travel insurance is cancellation cover, so you need to sort out insurance *before* you book the holiday.

Planning ahead gives you time to shop around for a good price and to make sure the cover is right. But don't panic if you do tend to leave things until the last minute – many phone and Internet operators and stores can issue immediate cover.

Where to buy

Cheapest cover tends to be from companies that sell by phone or the Internet – see Table 14.3. Some of these are 'direct' insurance companies (that is, insurers selling direct to the public and not through intermediaries), while others are brokers/other intermediaries. Companies selling through several media often offer a discount (say, 5 per cent) if you buy online.

Travel agents and tour operators tend to be costly. Research by *Which?* has found that insurance from a travel agent or tour operator frequently costs at least three times more than cover you arrange yourself with a best-buy provider. However, from time to time travel agents and tour operators run 'free' travel insurance promotions. These are a good deal *provided* you are not paying over the odds for the holiday.

There are many other outlets, including supermarkets and stores (for example, Tesco, Boots, Argos), banks and the Post Office, which all sell travel insurance. They are worth checking out but are not necessarily the cheapest places to buy.

If you plan to participate in sports while abroad, check whether cover is included. If not, consider a specialist in sports-related travel cover, such as Fogg Travel Insurance, Leading Edge, Sportscover Direct or Worldwide Travel (see Travel insurance providers*).

If you will be backpacking or taking a gap year, try a specialist, such as Journeywise, Leading Edge, Options or Worldwide Travel (see Travel insurance providers).

Travel accident insurance, which is sometimes a freebie with credit cards, is not a substitute for proper travel insurance. Travel accident insurance only pays out if you are injured or die as a result of an accident while travelling.

Many cheap insurance deals are aimed at people who are standard risks from the insurance company's point of view. If you are a higher than normal risk – for example, you have a health problem – you might not be eligible at all for a particular policy. However, other companies will ask for details and might still sell you insurance either at a higher price or with some restriction on cover – for example, no cover for claims directly related to the health problem. Bear in mind that it is a condition of insurance that you declare any health problems; claims could be refused if it turns out you didn't.

The box below lists travel insurance providers who came out well in a 2003 *Which?* survey.

Your rights and duties when shopping around for insurance

From 14 January 2005, the Financial Services Authority will regulate the sale of travel insurance. Until then, there is no compulsory system of regulation, but most insurers and many

---

Which? best buys in 2003

Single-trip policies:

- Direct Travel
- James Hampden
- Leading Edge
- Atlas Direct
- Family Care
- Worldwide Travel

Annual policies:

- Family Care
- Direct Travel
- James Hampden
- TravelPlan Direct
- Atlas Direct
- Flexicover Direct

intermediaries belong to the General Insurance Standards Council (GISC)★. Its members must abide by a code of practice. Many have also agreed to abide by a code of selling practice set out by the Association of British Insurers.

Among other things, the code requires that the person selling you insurance makes sure as far as possible that the policy is suitable for you and points out any significant or unusual conditions and any significant conditions you must meet. In particular, this includes warning you that you have a duty to disclose anything which might affect the insurer's offer of cover – for example, information about any pre-existing health conditions.

Under the code, if you buy by phone, you will normally have a 14-day cooling-off period from the time you receive the policy documents within which you can change your mind.

GISC members must have formal complaints procedures and belong to an independent complaints body – either the Financial Ombudsman Services★ or the GISC Dispute Resolution Facility.

Useful contacts

The websites included in this guide are ones that we found useful, interesting or popular. Many more websites are out there; we make no pretence at providing comprehensive coverage, and inclusion in this guide in no way endorses any product provided.

Banking Code
From your bank or building society or from the Banking Code Standards Board, 33 St James's Square, London SW1Y 4JS
Tel: 020-7661 9694 *www.bankingcode.org.uk*

British Insurance Brokers' Association (BIBA)
For a list of brokers in your area, contact BIBA, 14 Bevis Marks, London EC3A 7NT
Tel: 020-7623 9043 *www.biba.org.uk*

British Red Cross
For local branch, see phone book or *www.redcross.org.uk*

Car insurance providers that offer good deals for young people
- **Direct Choice** Tel: (0845) 128 5285 *www.directchoice.co.uk*
- **Endsleigh** Tel: (0800) 028 3571 See *Yellow Pages* for local branch or *www.endsleigh.co.uk*
- **Tesco** Tel: (0845) 300 4400 *www.tescofinance.com*

Car sharing
- *www.freewheelers.co.uk*
- *www.liftshare.com*
- *www.nationalcarshare.co.uk*
- *www.studentcarshare.com*
- some universities and local authorities promote local schemes

Citizens Advice Bureau
For local bureau, see phone book or *www.citizensadvice.org.uk*. For online information, see *www.adviceguide.org.uk*

Community Legal Service
Tel: (0845) 608 1122 *www.justask.org.uk*

Consumer Credit Counselling Service
Tel: (0800) 138 1111 *www.cccs.co.uk*

Credit-reference agencies
- **Call Credit** PO Box 491, Leeds LS3 1WZ Tel: (0870) 060 1414 *www.callcredit.plc.uk*
- **Equifax** PO Box 1140, Bradford, BD1 5US *www.econsumer.equifax.co.uk*
- **Experian** PO Box 8000, Nottingham NG1 5GX Tel: (0870) 241 6212 *www.uk.experian.com*

Department for Education and Skills (DfES)
Student Support Information Line: (0800) 731 9133 *www.dfes.gov.uk*

Employment tribunal
See phone book or *www.employmenttribunals.gov.uk*

Energywatch
Tel: (0845) 906 0708 *www.energywatch.org.uk*

Ethical Investment Research Service (EIRIS)
80–84 Bondway, London SW8 1SF Tel: 020-7840 5700 *www.eiris.org*

Financial Ombudsman Service (FOS)
South Quay Plaza, 183 Marsh Wall, London E14 9SR Tel: (0845) 080 1800 *www.financial-ombudsman.org.uk*

Financial Services Compensation Scheme (FSCS)
7th Floor, Lloyds Chambers, 1 Portsoken Street, London E1 8BN Tel: 020-7892 7300 *www.fscs.org.uk*

Financial Services Authority (FSA) comparative tables
FSA Consumer Helpline: (0845) 606 1234 *www.fsa.gov.uk/tables*

Fund supermarkets

- **Ample** *www.iii.co.uk*
- **CharcolOnline** *www.charcolonline.co.uk*
- **Chase de Vere** *www.chasedevere.co.uk*
- **Egg** *www.egg.com*
- **FundsNetwork** *www.fidelity.co.uk*
- **Hargreaves Lansdown** *www.hargreaveslansdown.co.uk*

General Insurance Standards Council (GISC)

110 Cannon Street, London EC4N 6EU Tel: (0845) 601 2857
www.gisc.co.uk

Independent Financial Adviser (IFA) – to find one

- **IFA Promotion** Tel: (0800) 085 3250 *www.unbiased.co.uk*
- **Institute of Financial Planning** Tel: (0117) 945 2470 *www.financialplanning.org.uk*
- **Matrix Data UK IFA Directory** *www.ukifadirectory.co.uk*
- **Society of Financial Advisers** Chartered Insurance Institute Tel: 020-8989 8464 *www.sofa.org*

Inland Revenue

- For information on all aspects of tax, see *www.inlandrevenue. gov.uk*
- For local office, see phone book or *www.inlandrevenue.gov.uk/ local*
- Helpline for the Newly Self-employed: (0845) 915 4515 *www.inlandrevenue.gov.uk/startup*

Investment Management Association (IMA)

Information Line: 020-8207 1361 *www.investmentuk.org*

Jobcentre Plus

For local office, see phone book or *www.jobcentreplus.gov.uk*

Local authority/Local education authority

See phone book under the name for your local authority. If you don't know the name, ask at your local public library

Local Education and Library Board (Northern Ireland)

For local board see phone book or *www.student-support.org.uk*

Moneyfacts
- Try larger public reference libraries for current issue
- Subscriptions Tel: (0870) 2250 100
- Online information *www.moneyfacts.co.uk*
- Faxback services, for example, savings accounts (0906) 076 0711, National Savings & Investments (0906) 076 0712

Money Management
- Single copies from larger newsagents
- Subscriptions/back issues Tel: 020-8606 7545

National Debtline
Tel: (0808) 808 4000 *www.nationaldebtline.co.uk*

National Minimum Wage
Helpline: (0845) 6000 678

National Savings & Investments (NS&I)
Post Offices Tel: (0845) 964 5000 *www.nsandi.com*

Personal finance websites
- *http://news.ft.com/yourmoney*
- *www.fsa.gov.uk/consumer*
- *www.moneyextra.com*
- *www.moneyfacts.co.uk*
- *www.moneysupermarket.com*
- *www.support4learning.co.uk*
- *www.youngmoney.com*

Save Energy
Energy Efficiency Helpline: (0845) 727 7200 *www.saveenergy. co.uk*

Search engines
- *www.alltheweb.com*
- *www.altavista.com*
- *www.google.com*
- *www.lycos.com*
- *www.yahoo.com*

Social Security Office

See phone book under entry for your local authority. State benefits for people of working age are administered by *Jobcentre Plus* (see above)

St John Ambulance

For local branch see phone book or *www.sja.org.uk*

Student Awards Agency for Scotland

Tel: (0845) 111 1711 *www.student-support-saas.gov.uk*

Student Finance Direct

www.studentsupportdirect.co.uk

Student Loans Company

Tel: (0800) 405010 *www.slc.co.uk*

Student office and student union

- Ask at the administration department for your college or university
- National Union of Students *www.nus.org.uk*

Student possessions insurance providers

- **Bank of Scotland** Tel: (0845) 723 3343 *www.bankofscotlandhalifax.co.uk*
- **Endsleigh** Tel: (0800) 0283571 *www.endsleigh.co.uk*
- **HSBC** Tel: (0800) 277377 *www.ukpersonal.hsbc.com*
- **Royal & Sun Alliance (More Than)** Tel: (0800) 783 5657 *www.royalsunalliance.co.uk*
- **Saxon** Tel: (0871) 230 6000 *www.saxoninsurance.com*

Switch with Which?

www.switchwithwhich.co.uk

Tax Office

See *Inland Revenue* above

Trading Standards Office

For local office, see phone book under name of your local authority or *www.tradingstandards.gov.uk*

Travel insurance providers
Backpacking/gap-year travel insurance specialists

- Journeywise Tel: (0870) 876 6969 *www.journeywise.co.uk*
- Leading Edge Tel: (01892) 836622 *www.leadedge.co.uk*
- Options Tel: (0870) 876 7878 *www.optionsinsurance.co.uk*
- Worldwide Tel: (01892) 833338 *www.worldwideinsure.com*

Providers that were Which? best buys in 2003

- Atlas Direct Tel: 020-7609 5000 *www.atlasdirect.net*
- Direct Travel Tel: (01903) 812345 *www.direct-travel.co.uk*
- Family Care Tel: (0870) 556 1224
- Flexicover Direct Tel: (0870) 990 9292 *www.flexicover.co.uk*
- James Hampden Tel: (01530) 416369 *www.jameshampden.com*
- Leading Edge Tel: (01892) 836622 *www.leadedge.co.uk*
- TravelPlan Direct Tel: (0870) 774 7377 *www.travelplan-direct.com*

- Worldwide Tel: (01892) 833338 *www.worldwideinsure.com*

Sports travel insurance specialists

- Fogg Travel Insurance Tel: (01623) 631 1331 *www.fogginsure.co.uk*
- Leading Edge Tel: (01892) 836622 *www.leadedge.co.uk*
- Sportscover Direct Tel: (0845) 120 6400 *www.sportscoverdirect. com*
- Worldwide Tel: (01892) 833338 *www.worldwideinsure.com*

Travel money – advice on what type to take with you
www.travel-guide.com

Young Scot
www.youngscot.org

Index

babysitting 86, 90, 93
bank accounts 9–34
   automated transfers 10
   basic bank accounts 10–11, 19, 66, 67, 71
   cash withdrawals 11, 12–13, 18–20
   clearing period 15, 34
   current accounts 10, 12, 13
   customer complaints 17
   customer rights 16–17
   debt problems and 66–7, 71
   direct credits 33, 34
   freebies 13–14
   interest on 11, 12, 13
   online banking 12, 13, 15
   opening an account 14–16
   paying in 10, 13, 29–32, 33
   shopping around for 12–14
   statements 33–4
   telephone and postal accounts 13
   terms and conditions 15, 34
   youth accounts 10, 11
   see also direct debits; overdrafts; savings accounts; standing orders

bank drafts 29
bankruptcy 65
borrowing 42–50
   debt consolidation 67–8
   legal contract 42
   personal loans 45–6, 67
   repayments (table) 44
   secured loans 48
   sensible borrowing 47
   shop credit 47
   see also credit; credit cards; interest; overdrafts; store cards; student loans

budgeting 35–41, 66
building society accounts 72, 75, 77

car insurance 130–40
   buying 138–9
   cancellation period 140
   complaints and compensation 140
   comprehensive 132–3, 134, 136
   disclosure of material facts 139–40
   excesses and exclusions 133, 136
   no claims bonus 135–6, 137
   premiums 133–4
   shopping around for 136–8
   third party 132
   third party fire and theft 132, 136
car-boot sales 38
cash machines 11, 12–13, 18–20, 29, 33, 148
   abroad 148
cash withdrawals
   abroad 148, 149
   by cheque 26
   by credit card 56
   from cash machines 11, 12–13, 18–20, 148
   from Post Offices 13, 20
   from supermarkets 20
catalogue shopping 47–8
charity shops 38
cheques 26–8
   'account payee' 26
   'bounced' cheques 26, 34
   cheque guarantee cards 12, 26
   chequebooks 10, 12
   clearing 30, 34
   paying in 30
   post-dated cheques 27
   writing a cheque 26–7, 28

council tax 41, 64
credit
  credit file 49, 50, 69
  credit-reference agencies 49, 50
  credit-repair agencies 49, 69
  credit-scoring 49
  creditworthiness 48–9, 65
  fraud 50
  interest-free credit 47
  refusal 49–50
  see also borrowing
credit cards 51–62
  abroad 56, 141, 148–9, 151
  annual fees 56
  applying for 60
  cash withdrawals 51, 56
  cashback 58, 60
  chip and PIN cards 61
  choosing 57–60
  consumer protection 55, 61–2
  credit limits 51
  donation cards 57
  fraud 60–1, 153
  interest 46, 52, 54, 58
  Internet-based cards 60
  late payment fees 56
  lost and stolen cards 61
  missed repayments 64
  paying off 46, 52, 55
  perks 58
  retailer fees 52
  statements 52, 53
  switching 54, 55
  transferred balances 54, 55

debit cards 11, 21–2
  abroad 141, 148–9, 151
debt 47, 63–71
  bankruptcy 65
  county court judgments (CCJs)
    65
  creditors 66, 70–1
  dealing with 66–71
  debt consolidation 67–8
  debt-management companies 68–9
  help and advice 68
  non-priority debts 65, 66, 70
  priority debts 64, 66, 70
  students 117
  warning signs 63

direct debits 11, 24–5, 38, 39
discount schemes 39
driving
  car-sharing schemes 39
  fuel efficiency 39
  learners 131, 134, 135
  without insurance 131
  see also car insurance

Electron cards 11, 21
emergency fund 73, 74
energy conservation 39

food shopping 38
foreign currency 56, 141, 142–6
friendly society savings plans 81, 82
fuel bills 25, 38, 63, 64
fuel conservation 39

gas and electricity suppliers 38
gifts from parents 82

hire-purchase 64
holiday money 141–54
  black market currency 152
  credit and debit cards 56, 141,
    148–9, 151
  euro 150
  exchange rates 56, 143, 144–5, 147,
    149
  foreign currency 56, 141, 142–6
  hard currencies 150
  limits 150–1
  scams 152–3
  security 151–4
  traveller's cheques 141, 146–7

identity, proof of 15–16
income, boosting 40–1
income tax 76–7, 98–100
  new job 104–5
  PAYE 102–4
  personal allowances 40, 76,
    77, 99
  rates 77, 99
  rebates 100–1
  on savings and investments 76–7
  self-assessment 105
  tax codes 97, 103, 104
  tax-free income 76, 77, 98

insurance 118–40
    buildings insurance 122
    car insurance 130–40
    house contents insurance 119, 120,
        122, 126
    possessions insurance 118–29
    travel insurance 142, 155–66
interest
    annual equivalent rate (AER) 79
    annual percentage rate (APR) 43
    bank account interest 11, 12, 13
    compounding 79
    credit cards 46, 52, 54, 58
    equivalent annual rate (EAR) 43
    on loans 42, 46–7
    overdrafts 45
    savings and investments 79
    store cards 46
    student loans 115–16
Internet
    banking online 12, 13, 15
    hackers 62
    Internet-based credit cards 60
    personal finance sites 57
    shopping online 11, 21, 22
ISAs 73, 77, 78

jobs 86–93
    below school-leaving age 86–8, 89, 90
    breaks and holidays 89
    contracts of employment 91
    hours of work 88–9
    illegal work 87
    national minimum wage 90–1
    pay statements 91, 94–105
    PAYE 102–4
    self-employment 105
    sick pay 89
    work permits 90
    written statements (terms and
        conditions) 91
Jobseeker's Allowance 41, 97, 101

Lebanese loop scam 20
loans see borrowing

magistrates' court fines 64
MasterCard 51
Moneyfacts 12, 57–8
mortgage payments 63, 64

National Insurance 40, 96–7, 101–2,
    105, 116
national minimum wage 90–1
National Savings and Investments 72,
    73, 76
    Children's Bonus Bonds 80, 82
    Investment Account 79–80
    Premium Bonds 80–1

overdrafts 10, 12, 18–19, 45, 63
    authorised 12, 45
    equivalent annual rate (EAR) 43
    free overdrafts 12, 45
    interest and charges 45
    unauthorised 12, 45

P45 105
PAYE 102–4
payments
    in advance 25
    by bank draft 29
    by cheque 26–8
    by debit card 21–2, 39
    by direct debit 24–5, 38
    by standing order 23–4
    over the Internet 11, 21, 22
    over the phone 11, 21
pensions 73, 74, 84–5
    occupational pension schemes 84,
        85, 97–8
    personal pensions 84, 85
    stakeholder pension schemes 84, 85
    state basic pension 101, 116
personal identification numbers
    (PINs) 18, 20, 21, 60
    changing 23
    chip and PIN credit cards 61
    security 23
personal loans 45–6, 67
possessions insurance 118–29
    accidental damage cover 124
    all-risks cover 120, 122, 124, 156–7,
        160
    buying 127
    cancellation period 128
    complaints and compensation 128–9
    cover 120–2
    disclosure of material facts 127–8
    excesses and exclusions 122–4
    indemnity basis 123

new-for-old basis 123
premiums 124–5
rented property 119
shopping around for 125–6
single-item limit 123, 126
university halls of residence 120
Post Office cash withdrawals 13, 20

renting 38
failure to pay rent 63, 64
insurance-with-rent scheme 119
Rent-a-Room Scheme 42
subletting 42

savings and investments 72–85
choosing 73, 77–85
ethical investments 84
interest 79
long-term goals 75
pensions 73, 74, 84–5
reasons for saving 72–5
risk 75, 76
savings accounts 10, 13, 72, 73, 74, 75, 77–8
short-term goals 75–6
stock-market investments 73, 74
taxation 76–7
see also individual investments
Scottish bank notes 145
'skimming' 60–1, 153
Solo cards 11, 21
sports insurance 160–1, 164
standing orders 11, 23–4
state benefits 36, 40–1
statutory school-leaving age 86, 88
store cards 46, 54, 63
student loans 77, 107, 111–14
applying for 114
'income contingent' 114
interest 115–16
maximum loans 107, 112

paying off 114, 116
writing off 116
students 106–17
accommodation 107, 108–9
bank accounts 12, 45
and burglaries 118
debts 117
expenditure 107, 108, 109
financial support schemes 111–15
graduate prospects 107
grants and bursaries 114
halls of residence 119–20
income 107–8
insurance 119–20, 125
paid work 100, 115
parental financial contribution 109–10, 113, 115, 116
top-up fees 110–11
tuition fees 109–11
supermarket cashback scheme 20

tax
capital gains tax 76
non-taxpayers 76, 100
tax years 94
see also income tax
telephone bills 25, 38, 64
telephone shopping 11, 21
travel
medical treatment 157–8
see also holiday money
travel insurance 142, 155–66
traveller's cheques 141, 146–7
TV licence 64

unit trusts 73, 75, 82–3

Visa 51

working see jobs